MAN AS SPIRIT, SOUL, AND BODY:

A Study of Biblical Psychology

By
John B. Woodward, D.Min.

Published by
Grace Fellowship International
P. O. Box 368
Pigeon Forge, TN 37868 USA

GraceFellowshipIntl.com
GraceNotebook.com
BiblicalPsychology.com
Phone: (865) 429-0450
john@gracenotebook.com

ISBN 1-931527-63-6

Cover Design by:
Beacon University
Columbus, GA

Printed by
Lightning Source Inc.
1246 Heil Quaker Blvd.
La Vergne, TN 37086 USA

Scripture quotations (unless indicated otherwise) are from
The Holy Bible, New King Janes Version
© 1982 by Thomas Nelson, Inc.

Library of Congress Cataloging-in-Publication Data

Woodward, John B. (John Bradford), 1955-
Man as spirit, soul, and body: a study of biblical psychology/
by John B. Woodward Jr.—2nd ed., rev.
p. cm.
Includes bibliographical references.
ISBN 1-931527-63-6 (pbk. : alk. paper)
1. Bible—Psychology. 2. Christianity—Psychology. 3. Psychology—Religious. I. Title.
BS645.W66 2007
233'.5—dc22
                                        2007015511

Acknowledgements

Most of the research and first draft of this book were done while I served as senior pastor of Winona Gospel Church, Stoney Creek Ontario. I began the project after about nine years of pastoral ministry there, during which time I repeatedly observed the value of a clear model of man in guiding parishioners in their spiritual journey. I thank the church for their loving support during my pastorate and after my transition to full time counseling and training with Grace Fellowship International in Tennessee.

A big thanks goes to my friend and counseling mentor, Charles Solomon. His writings reminded me of the relevance of this book's theme. I appreciate learning from his personal life and from his extensive clinical experience.

I also am grateful to Gerry Dilbeck, Cathy Solomon, John Norman and Cary Lantz for their editing assistance.

Research requires access to major libraries. I thank the following educational institutions for their libraries and staff: McMaster University (Hamilton, ON), Heritage College and Seminary (Cambridge, ON), Brock University and Concordia Lutheran Theological Seminary (St. Catharines, ON), Luther Rice University (Lithonia, GA), and Baptist Bible College and Graduate School (Clark Summit, PA).

My family has helped me in countless ways through their love, patience, and understanding. My parents and grandparents sponsored most of my college and seminary training. I hope this book will be a token of good stewardship of the investment they—and my teachers—have made in my life. To my wife, Linda, thank you for being a wonderful wife and partner in ministry.

Now to Him who is able to keep you from stumbling,
And to present you faultless
Before the presence of His glory with exceeding joy,
To God our Savior, Who alone is wise,
Be glory and majesty, Dominion and power,
Both now and forever. Amen (Jude 24,25).

Table of Contents

Foreword

Prior to Dr. Woodward's joining G.F.I. in 2001 and while yet a pastor in Canada, I believe our Lord prompted me to suggest that he do his research paper for his doctorate on biblical anthropology, with his emphasis being trichotomy. In recent church history, those espousing this position have done little published research on this vital topic, though the Scriptures are not silent in this regard.

This has resulted in defaulting this crucial area to those holding to dichotomy, monism or those who are so generous as to be multichotomous! Our consuming interest is to show how the model of man may be used to teach the doctrine of sanctification, since this is our focus in ministry. The trichotomous position, as delineated in 1 Thessalonians 5:23 and Hebrews 4:12, is intrinsic to our model of counseling/discipleship. That being the case, it is a great blessing to have a scholarly, as well as scriptural, apologetic for the model we have been using since the inception of our ministry in 1970.

Since my graduate studies were in counseling and education instead of theology, I am more than a little thankful that God sent and burdened Dr. Woodward to address this need. Though I did not need a theological credential for God to honor my use of the tripartite model of man in my writing and ministry, this book provides support to those who are seeking valid research on which to base their understanding of biblical psychology.

Having said all of this, I am not unaware that the dichotomous position is accorded the ranking of primacy by most evangelical Christian theologians. However, the sanctification message clarified by trichotomy was used by the Lord to revolutionize my life in 1965. Therefore, I have staked my professional reputation—as well as my temporal subsistence in ministry—on this model of man. God has honored this sanctification/counseling message with transformed lives around the world and has used this foundation to unlock the way to victory for many believers.

A person's having a spirit as a distinct functioning part is absolutely essential to a scriptural explanation of what was crucified, as well as what was regenerated. Since it is our intent to define our terms and the inner functioning of man from Scripture, rather than psychology, our model must also be anchored in Scripture. This makes it possible for a believer intelligently to cooperate with the Holy Spirit as He transforms the life to the glory of the Lord Jesus.

Thus, I heartily endorse this treatise on trichotomy without concern for a unanimous endorsement from academia. I am convinced that this volume is a major contribution to the cause of Christ as a foundation for Spirit-empowered living and ministry.

Charles R. Solomon, Ed. D.
Author of *Handbook to Happiness*

This book fills a unique niche in the emerging field of Christian discipleship counseling. Woodward takes on a challenging theological debate concerning the makeup of human beings and, in the process, builds a persuasive argument for the significant implications of a trichotomous view of human beings for the enterprise of Christian counseling. His fresh light on the subject is a thoughtful and invigorating invitation to pastors and professional and lay counselors alike, to rethink their assumptions about how we're made and how hurting people can be helped.

Cary Lantz, Ph. D.
Baptist Bible Graduate Scool, Clark Summit, PA

Introduction

The subtitle, a *Study in Biblical Psychology*, follows the precedent of book titles such as *A System of Biblical Psychology* (Franz Delitzsch) and *Biblical Psychology* (Oswald Chambers). Upon closer examination, the subject matter of man's material and immaterial makeup also relates to biblical anthropology. However, the titles just mentioned dealt with this same subject matter, so the following pages relate to biblical psychology as well. A second reason for the "psychology" designation is that the book's primary application in Part 2 relates to Christian counseling.

Back in 1901, *The Dictionary Of Philosophy And Psychology*, by James Mark Baldwin presented this definition:

> Biblical Psychology: Ger. *biblische psychologie*; Fr. p*sychologie biblique*; Ital. *psicologia biblica*. An integral portion of theological anthropology. It consists essentially of a discussion of man's entire constitution on the basis of Scripture declarations. Two main problems occur in it: (1) Is man composed of spirit (*pneuma*), soul (*psuche*), and body?—or (2) Is he composed of soul and body? The Greek Fathers, taken as a whole, adopted the former view; while the Latin Fathers, thanks partly to the emergence of Gnostic and other heresies, and partly to the poverty of the Latin language (*spiritus* and *anima* hardly conveying the sense of the Greek terms), tended to the latter view, or to a discreet silence. In the course of history, Biblical psychology has been rather elbowed out by dogmatics in the Western Church. The mystics raise the question of *pneuma* and *psuche* once more; and during the last 150 years more attention has been paid to it, especially in Germany, though systematic works are few.[1]

Therefore, this book will delve into the subject of man's nature under the category of biblical psychology.

Some who venture to read this material will do so to strengthen their belief that we are spirit, soul, and body. Trichotomy is assumed or taught in much devotional literature, evangelical preaching, and Christian counseling. It is hoped that this book will help confirm and clarify these convictions and provide some further evidence and rationale to defend them.

Others who will venture a closer look at the following chapters will be studying theology formally and are interested in the topic of man's constitutional makeup. Since this subject relates to each of us as people, the content seems relevant enough. However, teachers and students of theology will likely have read volumes of systematic theology authored by scholars with superior academic careers and intellectual gifts. Nevertheless, upon closer examination, many dichotomist theologians have basically restated conclusions from others in this field who have bypassed the trichotomy of man. Simply put, there were bigger fish to fry! The issue of the parts of man may have appeared to be of minor significance in this "queen of sciences."

I did not expect to re-examine biblical psychology/anthropology following my formal theological training. Yet, when this project of studying trichotomy got under way, it became obvious that a book length treatment of this important topic was long overdue. It seems that books such as Franz Delitzch's (1867) and John Heard's (1875) had no contemporary counterpart, and those two books have long been out of print.[2]

To offer further incentive for the reader to examine the following chapters, consider these questions about the makeup of man. What was the view of the early church? What did Martin Luther believe? Was Delitzsch (of the Keil-Delitzsch commentary fame) only a functional trichotomist? How has the lack of the adjective "soulish" or "soulical" in English obscured some of the biblical testimony for trichotomy? How can objections from other doctrinal viewpoints be answered? What practical difference does one's model of man make in understanding the Christian life? These topics are addressed in this book.

One last comment is due for those inquisitive enough to read an introduction. There will be a temptation for the theological student of another persuasion to glance through this material just to get some "grist for the mill" of academic debate. The plea is given here to take a higher road.

A sincere attempt has been made to respect the scholarship, motives, and intelligence of those holding alternate viewpoints. The conclusion reached in this study calls for an adjustment on the part of classical trichotomists that could help bridge the gap between contradictory perspectives. "Holistic trichotomy," at first glance, may appear to validate other viewpoints and thus detract from this book's main thesis: namely, *that the soul and spirit of man are ontologically distinct* (distinct in *being*). At the risk of alienating some classical trichotomists, the view of *holistic trichotomy* does not emphasize the compartmentalization of man; rather, his personhood is unified. The statement that "man is a spirit, who has a soul, and lives in a body" makes a greater separation than is needed or warranted by Scripture.

Each prominent viewpoint of man's constitutional makeup has an aspect of truth to it. This should invite more of a consensus, rather than permit each to run to his doctrinal corner. A human being is *one in personhood* (as in monism). He/she *has two separable elements*—the material and the immaterial (as in dichotomy). But, as this book contends, *the immaterial side of man has two ontologically distinct parts,* even as the biblical tabernacle and temple had two rooms. The soul and spirit are distinct, but never exist separately (nor did the rooms of the tabernacle and temple exist separately).

Is this discussion and terminology just a matter of semantics? The patient reader will discover how holistic trichotomy gives greater insights into redemption history, especially personal sanctification. One might go so far as to assert that the meaning of Romans chapters 5-8 will remain ellusive until the relevant terminology, parts, and faculties of man are clarified.

The reader is given permission to skip or scan the chapter on word studies if it seems too tedious. Yet, the chapter's summary and vocabulary lists (appendix A) will be useful in regard to the Hebrew and Greek biblical terms mentioned in this book.

I hope that theological scholars will verify the holistic trichotomy model and expand upon the preliminary implications that are delineated in this study.

[1] http://psychclassics.yorku.ca/Baldwin/Dictionary/defs/B1defs.htm

[2] Check www.BiblicalPsychology.com for these books online. Oswald Chambers' *Biblical Psychology* is in print, but has a wider scope and does not seek to evaluate alternative models of man.

PART 1

The Case for Man as Spirit, Soul, and Body

Chapter 1
Theological Models of Man's Makeup: Alternatives

Monism

Monism is the theological model that believes man is comprised of only one part. Although soul and spirit are identified as aspects of human nature, they do not consist of separable parts of man. Monism opposes both dichotomy and trichotomy, the usual evangelical models of man. As Philip Hefner contends, "Contemporary understanding of the human being and the human personality structure do not allow either a dichotomous or a trichotomous view, except metaphorically."[1]

In his discussion of the models of man's constitutional nature, Millard Erickson (as a dichotomist) writes:

Monism insists that man is not to be thought of in any sense composed of parts or separate entities, but rather as a radical unity. In the monistic understanding, the Bible does not view man as body, soul, and spirit, but simply as a self. The terms sometimes used to distinguish parts of man are actually to be taken as basically synonymous. Man is never treated in the Bible as a dualistic being.[2]

Monism has been the trend in academic circles in the past century. Liberal theologians as well as neo-orthodox scholars have been advocating it. Wayne Ward summarized this trend by stating, "Present theological and psychological emphasis is almost altogether upon the fundamental wholeness or unity of man's being..."[3]

This monistic perspective is also held by some evangelical scholars. Bruce Milne stated:

Today the dichotomy/trichotomy issue has been largely super-seded by an emphasis on the unity of the person. According to Scripture I do not consist of composite 'parts,' whether two or three; I am a psychosomatic unity.[4]

Likewise, Anthony Hoekema avoids the use of the terms "dichotomy" because it de-emphasizes man's essential unity:

> We must reject the term "dichotomy" as such, since it is not an accurate description of the biblical view of man. The word itself is objectionable...It therefore suggests that the human person can be cut into two "parts." But man in this present life cannot be so cut...The Bible describes the human person as a totality, a whole, a unitary being.[5]

Erickson, Milne, and Hoekema all concede that man's immaterial part separates at the time of physical death, thus they actually hold to a form of dichotomy. Physical monism, however, requires the belief that the soul does not survive the death of the body. Some theologians reconcile this in their eschatology, teaching that the soul and body are recreated by God *ex nihilo* at the resurrection. This view is known as recreationism.

Some theologians advocate *spiritual* monism. Instead of seeing the body and soul as an individual physical monad, they see man as an indivisible spiritual monad. Thus, the body is regarded as an illusion, as *maya* in Hinduism. The strong influence of eastern religions in the west has found "Christian" counterparts: e.g., Christian Science, Process Theology, and Gnosticism.[6]

Roman Catholic tradition also supports a monistic view of man. Thomas Aquinas advocated a middle position between the dualism of Plato and the monism of Aristotle (who compared the body with lumber and the soul with an architectural plan). However, Aquinas did write that "man is composed of a spiritual and of a corporeal substance," and that the soul survives death.[7] But Catholic anthropology in the twentieth century regarded the survival of the soul after physical death as a mystery; man is regarded as an ontological unity. A catechism states,

The unity of the soul and body is so profound that one has to consider the soul to be the 'form' of the body; i.e. it is because of the spiritual soul that the body of matter becomes a living, human body; spirit and matter in man, are not two natures united, but rather their union forms a single nature.[8]

Monism is sometimes advocated on scientific grounds. Calvin Seerveld urges evangelicals to discard the outdated belief in body, soul, and spirit as parts of man's constitution. He bases man's identity on "the structured thrust of the whole," which he considers indivisible.[9] Yet, this bias against the distinctive soul of man seems due to its immaterial quality. As George Jennings noted, this contemporary preference by social scientists, anthropologists, and psychologists to abandon the concept of the soul is due to their inability to study the soul experimentally.[10] Jeffrey Boyd observed the trend in the Evangelical Theological Society of using "spirit" as a replacement for the term "soul," with a monistic emphasis on man's nature. He concluded that many theologians confess that they have not thought enough about the soul, therefore theological anthropology is an underdeveloped and neglected aspect of evangelical theology.[11]

A prominent example of a case for monism is *The Body*, by John A. T. Robinson. A representative of the Biblical Theology movement, this neo-orthodox scholar assumed a sharp distinction between Greek and Hebrew thought. He agreed with H. Wheeler Robinson's assessment of the Hebrew idea of personality—man as an animated body, not an incarnated soul. So Robinson affirmed, "Man is a unity, and this unity is the body as a complex of parts, drawing their life and activity from a breath soul, which has no existence apart from the body."[12] In his work on systematic theology, Millard Erickson identifies major arguments for monism and answers them effectively.

Without going into further detail in responding to monism, evangelicals should be satisfied to examine biblical passages that refute this position. A fundamental testimony against monism is the fact that man's soul continues to live after the body dies. This necessitates the doctrine of the soul as an element distinct from the physical body. The Old Testament refers to this when Rachel's soul departed (Gen 35:18), and Ecclesiastes speaks of man's spirit as returning to God after death (Eccl 3:21). In the New Testament, Christ promised the thief on the cross that they would be in Paradise that very day (Luke 23:43). Paradise would sharply contrast the condition and location of their crucified bodies. The apostle Paul refuted monism when he testified,

> For I am hard pressed between the two [whether to prefer longer physical life or martyrdom] having a desire to depart and be with Christ, which is far better. Nevertheless to remain in the flesh is more needful for you...We are confident, yes, well pleased rather to be *absent from the body* and to be present with the Lord (Phil 1:23,24; 2 Cor 5:8; cf. Heb 12:23; Rev 6:9).*

Other references also indicate the distinction between soul and body. Daniel testified that his spirit was grieved in the midst of his body (Dan 7:15). Jesus warned His disciples not to fear human persecutors: "And do not fear those who kill the body but cannot kill the soul..." (Matt 10:28). I. Howard Marshall admits that most current biblical scholars are embarrassed by the dualism in Matthew 10:28, preferring to minimize it.[13] Nevertheless, here a clear distinction is drawn between man's material and immaterial parts. Franz Delitzsch noted the scriptural case against monism:

> If...the conclusion be drawn that there subsists no essential distinction between soul and body, Scripture is diametrically opposed to this; for it bids us from the first page to look upon the *kosmos* dualistically, so also it bids us look at man...for the spirit...is something essentially different in its nature from matter. According to its representation, man is the synthesis of two absolutely distinct elements.[14]

The apostle John made this clear in his blessing: "Beloved, I pray that you may prosper in all things and be in [physical] health, just as your *soul* prospers" (3 John 2).

These observations show that, although the Scriptures value man's unity of personhood, there is an undeniable distinction of parts in his being. Further refutations of monism come from some of the biblical arguments for dichotomy.

Man As Spirit, Soul, and Body

Dichotomy

This view of human nature sees man's constituent elements as two—the physical and the spiritual. The term "dichotomy" derives two Greek roots: *diche*, meaning "twofold" or "into two"; and *temnein*, meaning "to cut." Augustus Strong states this view:

> Man has a two-fold nature,—on the one hand material, on the other immaterial. He consists of body, and of spirit, or soul. That there are two, and only two, elements in man's being, is a fact to which consciousness testifies. This testimony is confirmed by Scripture, in which the prevailing representation of man's being is that of dichotomy.[15]

Just as there are two varieties of monism (physical and spiritual), there are two varieties of dualism (Platonic and holistic). Plato's teaching is representative of Greek dualism. Milne noted,

> Plato saw man as two separable parts, body and soul; at death the soul was liberated, the divine spark in man passing from its shadowy life in the prison-house of the body to the real world beyond physical dissolution.[16]

Thus, Greek philosophers regarded the body as intrinsically bad, in contrast to the soul. (This negative attitude toward the body is seen in the criticism of the doctrine of the resurrection by the philosophers of the Areopagus in Acts 17:32.) Descartes' form of dualism likewise emphasized the separate substances of body and soul.

Holistic dualism maintains the distinction in man's constitution while emphasizing his unity. This view goes by a variety of titles such as "minimal dualism" (C. S. Evans), "interactive dualism" (Gordon Lewis), "conditional unity" (Millard Erickson), or "psychosomatic unity" (Anthony Hoekema). Lewis and Demarest advocate this position:

> To sum up the doctrine of humanness ontologically,...the whole person is a complex unity composed of two distinct entities, soul and body, intimately interacting with one another...an interacting dichotomy.[17]

How does dichotomy differ from the dualism of Plato? Lewis and Demarest further clarify this.

> The body is not the blameworthy cause of human evil, the inner self is. The existence of the naked spirit after death is an intermediate and incomplete state, not the eternal state. In the eternal state humans are not immortal souls only, but spirits united with resurrection bodies...[The body] is not the prison house of the soul but its instrument. The body is not less real than the soul.[18]

If Platonism viewed the body and soul as joined in a bad marriage, holistic dualism sees them in a harmonious one.

Strong arranged the scriptural support for dichotomy in four observations. First he noted the record of man's creation (Gen 2:7), in which, as a result of the inbreathing of the divine Spirit, indicates that the body becomes possessed and vitalized by a single principle—the living soul.[19] Secondly, Strong observed texts in which the soul (or spirit) is distinguished, both from the divine Spirit—from whom it proceeded—and from the body which it inhabits (Num 12:1; 16:22; 1 Cor 2:11). Various texts distinguish the soul, or spirit of man, from the body (Gen 35:18; 1 Kgs 17:21; James 2:26). Thirdly, Strong noted the interchangeable use of the terms "soul" and "spirit": they both are used to refer to emotions (Gen 41:8; Psalm 42:6), Jesus giving of His life (Matt 20:28; 27:50), and the intermediate state of man (Heb 12:23; Rev 6:9). Fourthly, Strong pointed to the mention of body and soul (or spirit) as together constituting the whole person (3 John 2; 1 Cor 5:3; Matt 10:28).[20]

Berkhof gave an historical survey of this doctrinal view and then endorsed dichotomy. He first noted the biblical emphasis on the unity of man's person:

> While recognizing the complex nature of man, it [the Bible] never represents this as resulting in a twofold subject in man. Every act of man is seen as an act of the whole man. It is not the soul but man that sins; it is not the body but man that dies; and it is not merely the soul, but man, body and soul, that is redeemed by Christ.[21]

Berkhof then proceeded to explore the nature of man's duality. Occasionalism (suggested by Cartesius) is rejected because it proposes that matter and spirit each function according to their own peculiar laws; these laws are so different that joint action of soul and body are impossible without divine intervention. Another theory of the relationship of soul and body is parallelism (proposed by Leibnitz). This view also assumes that there is no direct interaction between the material and spiritual, yet God is not the source of the apparent harmony of the two in man's activity. Instead, there is a pre-established harmony so that they act in concert with each other; when the body moves, the soul has a corresponding movement. Berkhof affirmed dichotomy which he called realistic dualism: "...body and soul are distinct substances which do interact, though their mode of interaction escapes human scrutiny and remains a mystery for us."[22]

To substantiate dichotomy (instead of trichotomy), the soul and spirit are defined as denoting the same immaterial part of man, yet with distinct connotations. Dichotomist theologians have different ways of clarifying this distinction. Gordon Clark is representative of those who identify "soul" as the combination of body and spirit. Commenting on Genesis 2:7 he writes,

> God constructed man out of two elements: the dust of the ground and His own breath. The combination is *nephesh* ...In the Old Testament the term "soul" designates the combination as a whole, not just one of the components.[23]

Strong defined *soul* as "the immaterial part of man, viewed as an individual and conscious life, capable of possessing and animating a physical organism." *Spirit* is then described as this same immaterial part, "viewed as a rational and moral agent, susceptible of divine influence and indwelling.[24] He elaborated on these contrasts:

> The *pneuma*, then, is man's nature looking Godward, and capable of receiving and manifesting the *pneuma hagion* [Holy Spirit]; the *psuche* is man's nature looking earthward, and touching the world of sense...[man's] immaterial part, while possessing duality of powers, has unity of substance.[25]

This perspective of dichotomists, regarding soul/spirit, was summarized by J. O. Buswell:

> As *soul* designates the non-material personal being, usually when there is some reference to his body or his earthly connections...so the word *spirit* designates a personal being in those circumstances in which reference to earthly connections and ordinary human function is absent.[26]

The understanding of spirit as the higher aspect of man's immaterial being is a consistent feature of dichotomist theologians; they reject, however, the ontological distinction between soul and spirit.

Multifaceted

In the attempt to discern the parts of man, a variation on the views described above is that man has a plurality of aspects that defy a decisive distinction of spirit, soul, and body. In addition to studying *psuche* and *pneuma*, other aspects of man also need to be identified and incorporated into man's makeup.[27] The following is a sample list of such faculties with brief definitions.

Heart. The Hebrew term is *leb*; the Greek term is *kardia.* There are over 700 biblical references to the heart of man. "Keep your heart with all diligence, For out of it *spring* the issues of life" (Prov 4:23; cf. John 14:1). Easton's Dictionary states, "According to the Bible, the heart is the centre not only of spiritual activity, but of all the operations of human life."

Conscience. The Greek word is *suneidesis.* The New Testament refers to the conscience about twenty eight times. The author of Hebrews implored, "Pray for us; for we are confident that we have a good conscience, in all things desiring to live honorably" (Heb 13:18; cf. Rom 2:15). It is "that faculty of the mind, or inborn sense of right and wrong, by which we judge of the moral character of human conduct" (Easton).

Mind. "Mind" occurs eighty eight times in the NKJV Bible. The Greek words translated thus are *nous, dianoia,* and *sunesis.* "Therefore gird up the loins of your mind, be sober, and rest your hope fully upon the grace that is to be brought to you at the revelation of Jesus Christ" (1 Pet 1:13; cf. Rom 12:2). This refers to the faculty of thought and reasoning.

Will. The Greek term is *thelema.* This refers to man's faculty of volition "...who were born, not of blood, nor of the will of the flesh, nor of the will of man, but of God" (John 1:13: cf. 1 Cor 7:37).

To these terms could be added other aspects of man known from personal awareness and scriptural designation: emotions, imagination, affections, etc. *The multifaceted view, however, sidesteps the issue of whether the spirit is a distinguishable "part" of man.* This explanation lumps all these spiritual and psychological terms into one category of the non-material side of man or as "man."

The current academic climate—even among evangelicals—favors the unity of man to the point of disparaging dichotomy and/or trichotomy as "reductionistic." In a recent textbook on Christian counseling, the authors claim,

> People must always be thought of and related to as a complex unity. Any effort to describe persons in a compartmentalized way is simply an accommodation to our limited reasoning abilities...no absolute division of human beings is evident in the text of Scripture.[28]

However, the scriptural evidence cited above to refute monism applies to the monistic multifaceted view as well. The ontological distinction of man's parts precedes the discussion of what should be emphasized in relating to people in counseling. (This principle will be explored in chapter 8.)

The issues differentiating the multifaceted view and trichotomy can be illustrated in an analysis of the tabernacle (Exodus chapters 25-31). This worship structure had a variety of furnishings including the lampstand, the table of showbread, the altar of incense, the ark of the covenant, the mercy seat, and the cherubim. In addition to these items in the tabernacle was the ministering priesthood. How many rooms were in this tabernacle? The two rooms were the Holy Place and the Holy of Holies. Understanding the distinction between these two is essential to perceive the placement of the furnishings and to regulate the high priest's role on the Day of Atonement. What is the difference between a lampstand and the Holy Place? Although there is an overlap of meaning (because the former was *in* the latter), the lampstand was a *furnishing* whereas the Holy Place was a *room.* Similarly, mind, will and emotions are faculties; the soul is part of man. The significance of the tabernacle as a scriptural symbol of man will be explored in more detail in the following chapters.

Summary

This chapter has surveyed the three alternative models of man's makeup, rejecting monism unequivocally. The case for dichotomy has earned it the status of being the majority position of evangelical theologians. In the next chapter we will examine the trichotomous view of man. As this model is presented and defended, the deficiencies of the models presented above should become more apparent.

*The NKJV translation is used for biblical quotations in this book because of its accuracy, current English, traditional style, and textus receptus manuscript usage. Italicized words are not implied (as in the NKJV Bible editions), but indicate emphasis added by this writer; bracketed comments in the book are inserted for clarification.

　　　　　　　　　　　　Man As Spirit, Soul, and Body

[1] Philip J. Hefner, *Forth Locus: The Creation*, in *Church Dogmatics*, ed. Carl E. Braaten and Robert W. Jenson (Philadelphia: Fortress Press, 1984), 334.

[2] Millard J. Erickson, *Christian Theology* (Grand Rapids: Baker Book House, 1983), 524.

[3] Everett F. Harrison, ed., *Baker's Dictionary of Theology* (Grand Rapids: Baker Book House, 1960), s.v. *Trichotomy*, by Wayne Ward, 531.

[4] Bruce Milne, *Know the Truth* (Downers Grove, IL: Inter Varsity Press, 1982), 97. Evangelicals Robert Pyne and Matthew Blackman advocate monism since they see dichotomy as reminiscent of Greek dualism and trichotomy as "faulty anthropology" ("A Critique of the Exchanged Life," *Bibliotheca Sacra*, 163 [2006]: 138,39,49). They appeal to scientific studies to buttress monism. However, issues such as man's soul/spirit distinction are beyond the realm of materialistic science. Revelation is required for definitive information on the spiritual realm (Heb 4:12). For a more detailed response to this article, see chapter 7 and a response paper at www.BiblicalPsychology.net.

[5] Hoekema, *Created in God's Image*, 209-10.

[6] Ibid., 212.

[7] Ibid., 209.

[8] *Catechism of the Catholic Church* (Liguori: Liguori Publications, 1994) 93; quoted in Boyd, "One's Self Concept in Biblical Theology," 209.

[9] Calvin Seerveld, "A Christian Tin Can Theory of Man," *Journal of the American Scientific Affiliation* 33 (1981): 74.

[10] George J. Jennings, "Some Comments on the Soul," *Journal of the American Scientific Affiliation* 19/1 (1967): 7-11.

[11] Jeffrey H. Boyd, "The Soul as Seen Through Evangelical Eyes," *Journal of Psychology and Theology* 23 (1995): 161-70.

[12] Erickson, *Christian Theology*, 526.

[13] Boyd, "One's Self Concept in Biblical Theology," *Journal of the Evangelical Theological Society* 40 (1997): 215.

[14] Franz Delitzsch, *A System of Biblical Psychology* (Edinburgh: T. & T. Clark, 1867), 104-105. Dallas Willard defines "spirit" as *unembodied personal power. The Spirit of the Disciplines* (San Francisco: Harper & Row), 64.

[15] Augustus H. Strong, *Systematic Theology* (Philadelphia: Judson Press, 1907), 485.

[16] Milne, *Know the Truth*, 97.

[17] Gordon R. Lewis and Bruce A. Demarest, *Integrative Theology* (Grand Rapids: Zondervan, 1990), 148-49, quoted by Boyd, "One's Self Concept in Biblical Theology," 211.

[18] Ibid.

[19] Strong, *Systematic Theology*, 485.

[20] Ibid.

[21] L. Berkhof, *Systematic Theology* (Grand Rapids: Eerdmans, 1939), 192.

[22] Ibid., 195.

[23] Gordon H. Clark, *The Biblical Doctrine of Man* (Jefferson, MD: The Trinity Foundation, 1984), 37.

[24] Strong, *Systematic Theology*, 486.

[25] Ibid.

[26] J. O. Buswell, *A Systematic Theology of the Christian Religion* (Grand Rapids: Zondervan, 1962), 1:240.

[27] Paul Enns, *Moody Handbook of Theology* (Chicago: Moody Press, 1989), 307.

[28] Harry Shields and Gary Bredfeldt, *Caring for Souls: Counseling Under the Authority of Scripture* (Chicago: Moody Press, 2001), 80-81.

Chapter 2
Theological Models of Man's Makeup: Trichotomy

This chapter will describe the model of man this book seeks to clarify, support, and defend. Hebrews 4:12 indicates that the soul/spirit distinction is not obvious. Only the Word of God can reveal their subtle, yet important distinctives. A definition of trichotomy is given by Paul Enns:

> Trichotomy comes from the Greek *tricha*, "three," and *temno*, "to cut." Hence, man is a three part being, consisting of body, soul, and spirit. The soul and spirit are said to be different both in function and substance.[1]

The distinction of soul and spirit, however, does not require an emphasis on disunity of the human constitution. As recent dichotomists emphasize the unity of man's nature, so the trichotomist can value this unity. J. B. Heard reflected this balance in his definitive work, *The Tripartite Nature of Man*:

> We may distinguish in idea, as we shall presently see Scripture does, between body, soul, and spirit; but to suppose that either can act without the other, or to suppose, for instance, that the unsouled body, or the disembodied soul, or lastly, the unsouled spirit, can act by itself, is to assume something which neither reason nor revelation warrants... The facts of consciousness are all against such a trichotomy as would divide as well as distinguish the natures in man."[2]

Thus, the perception of three parts of man's makeup does not require a de-emphasis on man's unity of personhood. Likewise, trichotomy agrees with most of the biblical propositions of dichotomist theologians. L. T. Holdcroft acknowledges this common ground as he defines trichotomy:

> The trichotomist divides the non-material element of the human into two parts, so that with the body, he views humans as three-part or tripartite beings. In the traditional language, the trichotomist usually speaks of: body, soul and spirit. In most cases, the trichotomist freely accepts the dichotomist's Scriptures [interpretations] and probably most of his arguments. The two viewpoints agree that man is both material and non-material, and therefore the trichotomist does not so much object to what has been done [by dichotomists], but rather simply seeks to proceed a step further. [3]

Articulations of Trichotomy

It has been noted that recent scholarship favors a monistic view of man, although evangelical scholarship is usually dichotomist. Trichotomy has, nevertheless, been popular among more fundamental Bible teachers since its resurgence in the 19th century.   One example of this is the following note from the *Scofield Reference Bible*. Commenting on 1 Thessalonians 5:23, it states,

> Man is a trinity. That the human soul and spirit are not identical is proved by the facts that they are divisible (Heb 4:12), and that the soul and spirit are sharply distinguished in the burial and resurrection of the body...(1 Cor 15:44).[4]

G. H. Pember wrote of the distinctive functions of man's three parts:

> Now the body we may term the sense-consciousness, the soul the self-consciousness, and the spirit the God-consciousness. For the body gives us the five senses; the soul comprises the intellect which aids us in the present state of existence, and the emotions which proceed from the senses; while the spirit is our noblest part, which came directly from God, and by which alone we are able to apprehend and worship Him.[5]

Typically, trichotomists would recognize the spirit of man as that which distinguishes him from animals (not just qualitatively, but substantively). For example, defining the soul, the author of *Biblical Doctrine* wrote,

> The soul is the seat of the emotions and appetites. Plants, animals and man have bodies. Only animals and man have a soul; but only man has a spirit...There is a difference between the souls of man and the souls of animals...The soul of an animal dies with the animal, but man's soul never dies...The spirit of man is the seat of his [spiritual] intelligence (1 Cor 2:11). Animals do not possess [such] intelligence.[6]

The issue of animals not possessing a spirit has been challenged because the Hebrew word *ruach* [spirit] is occasionally used in reference to animals in the Old Testament. *Ruach* is used of animals in Genesis 7:15, Psalm 104:29, and Ecclesiastes 3:21. Evidently, in these three contexts *ruach* is used in the literal, physical sense of "breath." In the first case it is used as "breath [*ruach*] of life"—designating respiration of physical life in animals. *Ruach* is translated as "breath" in the Old Testament about twenty seven times. (However, if one takes those three references as proof that humans and animals both have a "spirit," it still must maintained that man's spirit is qualitatively higher due to his dignity as made in God's image.)

Some theologians who hold to a trichotomist view are not dogmatic; they state that the Scriptures can be interpreted to support both trichotomy and dichotomy. L. S. Chafer stated this in his *Systematic Theology*,

> The Bible supports both dichotomy and trichotomy. The distinction between soul and spirit is as incomprehensible as life itself, and the efforts of men to frame definitions must always be unsatisfactory.[7]

When it appears that Chafer will be non-committal on this issue, he goes on to note,

> Many have assumed that the Bible teaches only a dichotomy. Over against this is the truth that oftentimes these terms cannot be used interchangeably. At this point it may

be observed that there is the closest relation between the human spirit and the Holy Spirit—so close, indeed, that it is not always certain to which a reference is made in the sacred text...The Holy Spirit works in and through the human spirit, but this is not said of the human soul. "The Spirit itself beareth witness with our spirit" (Rom 8:16). A soul may be lost, but this is not declared of the spirit (Matt 16:26).[8]

Henry Theissen taught trichotomy with the recognition that the unseen side of man has two parts—spirit and soul. He summarized,

In other words, man's immaterial nature is looked upon as one nature, but composed of two parts. Sometimes the parts are sharply distinguished; at other times, by metonymy, they are used for the whole [immaterial] being.[9]

The Human Spirit

The dichotomist can concede that man's spirit is distinct as a faculty or function of the soul, but trichotomy affirms a more pronounced distinction. One of the most influential, scholarly cases for trichotomy was that of Franz Delitzsch in his *A System of Biblical Psychology*. Dichotomist scholars have sought to rationalize his departure from the two part model of man. They take various approaches to pay tribute to his work while maintaining a dichotomist view. For example, Buswell quoted Delitzsch, then interpreted his view:

It should be evident to the reader that in this quotation [from Delitzsch] the word "distinct" [soul from spirit] means functionally distinct and not substantively distinct, a distinction of "aspect," not of substance. There is nothing in Delitzsch's work to show that the difference between "soul" and "spirit" is other than a difference of functional names for the same substantive entity, the same kind of difference that obtains between "heart" and "mind."[10]

It is understandable why Buswell would assume Delitzsch was asserting only a *functional distinction* of spirit and soul. However, the quotes used were contrasting man's material

Man As Spirit, Soul, and Body

and immaterial elements. Such an interpretation, which seeks to nullify this German scholar's influential case for trichotomy, requires closer scrutiny.

In his book, Delitzsch identified the usual view of interpreting soul and spirit as different functional attributes, yet insists that biblical psychology affirms an ontological distinction between them:

> The *psuche* must be more than the form of existence, the individualization of the spirit; for Scripture certainly appropriates to the spirit and soul different functions, and often in juxtaposition. They must be distinguished even otherwise [more than by mere function]...[or else] a man would then not be able to speak of his spirit specially, and of his soul specially.[11]

Delitzsch also rejected another approach to removing the actual distinction between spirit and soul:

> Rather might spirit and soul be apprehended as only two distinct sides of one principle of life...But even this distinction is far from being sufficient for the case in question... The spirit is superior to the soul. The soul is its product, or, what is most expressive, its manifestation.[12]

The chapter Buswell quoted from is titled "True and False Trichotomy." Here Delitzsch interacted with various forms of both dichotomy and trichotomy, clearly advocating the latter:

> And as for the essential condition of man, I certainly agree entirely with the view that the spirit and soul of man are distinguished as primary and secondary, but not with the view that spirit and soul are substantially one and the same.[13]

Whereas dichotomists require trichotomists to assert the possibility of soul and spirit potentially separating (to prove their actual distinction), Delitzsch allowed for them to be only potentially independent:

> If any one would rather say that the soul is a Tertium, or third existence, not substantially indeed, but potentially independent, between spirit and body, but by its nature per-

taining to the side of the spirit, we have no objection to it.[14]

Delitzsch's conclusions are softened by dichotomists because he acknowledged the obvious; the distinction of the material and immaterial is more apparent and observable than the subtle distinctions between soul and spirit. He stated that soul and spirit are the same "nature" [element].[15] The difficulty of choosing accurate terms to express these delicate distinctions is evident. He looks to the relationship of the persons of the Trinity to parallel the distinction of man's two immaterial parts:

> [The soul] is not one and the same substance with the spirit, but a substance which stands in a secondary relation with it. It is of one nature with it...as the Son and the Spirit are of one nature with the Father, but not the same *hypostases*.[16]

In light of these representative quotes, Delitzsch's seminal book must be recognized as teaching the trichotomous view of man.

Heard published a thorough study of biblical psychology, defining and defending trichotomy. He also affirmed that the spirit is more than a function of the soul:

> The *pneuma* is, we admit, very closely joined to the *psuche*; but so is the *psuche* to the animal [physical] frame. If we can distinguish between soul and body, as all psychologists who are not materialists do; are we not bound equally to distinguish between soul and spirit? Consciousness is the common term which unites these three natures of man together...It is not, as dichotomists would say, that the spirit is only the reasonable soul exercised upon the inner world of the spirit instead of the outer world of the sense.[17]

C. A. Beckwith described the distinction of the human spirit as the divine principle of life in man; it is included in the soul, but distinct from it:

> The spirit is the condition, soul the manifestation of life. Whatever belongs to the spirit belongs to the soul also, but not everything that belongs to the soul belongs to the spir-

it...it does not suffice to speak of the inner being of man, now as the spirit, now as the soul; one must regard the spirit as the principle of the soul, the divine principle of life, included in but not identical with the individual.[18]

The human spirit is defined by Thomas Holdcroft as the animating principle which causes the man to be alive. God is the author of the human spirit (Num 27:16; Zech 12:1), and when the spirit is withdrawn, the body dies (Jas 2:26). The biblical references to *the spirit of man* in the New Testament are categorized by Holdcroft:

1) those that identify strictly the human principle of life and 2) those that identify the expression of that life in feelings, convictions and motivations. In this second usage many see an overlap between the role of the spirit and that which is commonly identified as the human soul. At least it is clear that the human soul is more than merely an impersonal life principle; it is a human life-principle that is distinctive and individually personal.[19]

Another example of this view that distinguishes spirit from soul is found in Oswald Chambers' lectures on biblical psychology: "The spirit is the essential foundation of man; the soul his peculiar essential form; the body his essential manifestation."[20] Expounding on the human spirit, he commented, "Remember, the whole meaning of the soul is to express the spirit, and the struggle of the spirit is to get itself expressed in the soul."[21] Yet the process of sanctification involves the whole person. Chambers stated,

God knows of no divorce whatsoever between the three aspects of the human nature, spirit, soul, and body; they must be at one, and they are at one either in damnation or in salvation.[22]

Watchman Nee expressed the doctrine of trichotomy in a methodical, extensive way in his three volume *The Spiritual Man.* Speaking of the importance of identifying the spirit, he wrote:

It is imperative that believers recognize a spirit exists within them, something extra to thought, knowledge, and imagination of the mind, something beyond affection, sensation and pleasure of the emotion, something additional to desire, decision and action of the will. This component is far more profound than these faculties. God's people not only must know that they possess a spirit; they also must understand how this organ operates—its sensitivity, its work, its power, its laws. Only in this way can they walk according to their spirit and not the soul or body of their flesh.[23]

Nee went on to identify and elaborate on three major faculties of man's spirit—that of intuition, conscience, and communion.

The Human Soul

The soul is described by the data of the biblical word studies which bring out its distinctive functions. The Scofield Reference Bible defined the human soul as the "seat of the affections, desires, and so of the emotions, and of the active will, the self."[24] T. Austin-Sparks (a British pastor who assisted Watchman Nee), wrote that,

[The soul is] the plane or organ of human life and communication...Thus, what is received by the spirit alone with its peculiar faculties is translated for practical purposes, firstly to the recipient himself, and then to other humans, by means of the soul. This may be an enlightened mind for truth (reason); a filled heart, with joy or love, etc., for comfort and uplift (emotion); or energized will for action or execution (volition).[25]

Heard affirmed the soul's faculty of free will:

Soul, or self-consciousness as the union point between spirit and body, was created free to choose to which of these two opposite poles [the flesh or the spirit] it would be attracted.[26]

Another representative of the Keswick movement, Jessie Penn-Lewis, quoted Tertullian, Pember, and Andrew Murray in support of trichotomy. She summarized the functions of the soul:

> We see that all these writers practically define the "soul" as the seat of the personality, consisting of the will and the intellect or mind; a personal entity standing between the "spirit" and the "body"—open to the outer world of nature and sense; the soul having power of choice as to which world shall dominate the entire man.[27]

(Penn-Lewis' writing preceded Watchman Nee's which elaborated on these themes primarily for the believers in China.)

Some trichotomists identify the soul as the phenomenon of the union of man's body and spirit. K. Liu wrote,

> The soul is the totality of the being, while the spirit is the immaterial vitality of the soul. The soul lives so long as the body is in contact with the spirit. The soul dies and is thus temporal while the spirit is never said to die and hence it must be immortal.[28]

This view is based primarily on the exegesis of Genesis 2:7 which describes the creation of man. However, this position encounters difficulty reconciling texts which describe the soul of man existing after death, but prior to the resurrection (Rev 6:9; 20:4; Matt 10:28)—although some may justify this concept through the implied intermediate body (Matt 17:3; Luke 16:24).

The faculty of man's affections seems equally applied to the soul and the spirit. This combination seems to correspond to the biblical usage of the "heart" when used metaphorically.[29] (The biblical data do not warrant seeing the heart as a constituent element in man, distinct from the soul or spirit.) Affections relate to one's values and are expressed through the moral imperative of love. Man is to not love the world system (in its opposition to God), but to love God and people. Love for God is to be with all of one's heart (Mark 12:30; cf. Chapter 3 and Appendix E).

The Human Body

The material part of man is the one most easily identified and described. Since it can be examined empirically, the nature of the body is described in the science of anatomy. In addition to scientific knowledge about the physical part of man, we have many references to it in Scripture, some of which are surveyed in the next chapter. Dichotomists and trichotomists agree on the nature of the body as man's material part; together they disagree with monism which does not distinguish the soul as an element distinct from the body. L. T. Holdcroft defines the body as a house or vehicle in which man lives and through which he performs activities on earth. He also notes some features that distinguish man's body from the animals, including his brain's capabilities, an opposable thumb, and an upright posture.[30]

Paul, the tentmaker, spoke of the mortal body as a tent:

For we know that if *our earthly house, this tent,* is destroyed, we have a building from God, a house not made with hands, eternal in the heavens. For in this we groan, earnestly desiring to be clothed with our habitation which is from heaven...For we who are in this tent groan, being burdened, not because we want to be unclothed, but further clothed, that mortality may be swallowed up by life" (2 Cor 5:1-4; cf. 2 Pet 1:13,14).

At death, the believer's soul and spirit go to heaven to be with God. Paul continued,

So we are always confident, knowing that while we are at home in the body we are absent from the Lord. For we walk by faith, not by sight. We are confident, yes, well pleased rather *to be absent from the body and to be present with the Lord* (2 Cor 5:6,8; cf. Phil 1:23).

The body will decompose after death. As God pronounced to Adam at the Fall, "...For out of it [the soil] you were taken; For dust you are, And to dust you shall return" (Gen 3:19).

Man is designed to use the body as a servant to his immaterial nature. In fallen man the body craves its own gratification, so self-discipline is required. Paul again testified, "But I discipline my body and bring it into subjection, lest, when I have preached to others, I myself should become disqualified" (1 Cor 9:27). In contrast to Platonic trichotomy, the material body was created as good (Gen 1:31). Sexual relations of a husband and wife are an important aspect of marriage (Gen 1:28; 1 Cor 7:3-5); and food is to be received with thanksgiving (1 Tim 4:3). The Christian is responsible to use his body as an instrument of righteousness (Rom 6:12,13), which is an essential aspect of progressive sanctification (1 Thes 4:3-5).

Summary

This basic description of trichotomy has demonstrated how it differs from the dichotomous, monistic, and multifaceted models of man. Scriptural summaries of the parts of man as spirit, soul, and body validate trichotomy. Some variation of definitions within the basic model have been noted. Chapter 6 will delve into this view further, proposing some clarifying principles which we will call "holistic trichotomy." To further substantiate the distinction of spirit, soul, and body, the next chapter will survey the biblical use of their corresponding terms.

[1] Paul Enns, *The Moody Handbook of Theology* (Chicago: Moody Press, 1989), 307. Note the meaning of trichotomy stated by Cremer: "Apparently, then, the relationships may be summed up, *soma*, body, and *pneuma*, spirit may be separated, *pneuma* and *psuche*, soul, can only be distinguished" – C. F. Hogg and W. E. Vine, *The Epistles to the Thessalonians* (Fincastle, VA: Scripture Truth Book Co., 1914), 207.

[2] J. B. Heard, *The Tripartite Nature of Man: Spirit, Soul and Body* (Edinburgh: T. & T. Clark, 1875), 116, 120.

[3] L. Thomas Holdcroft, *Anthropology: A Biblical View* (Clayburn, BC: Cee Picc, 1990), 20.

[4] *The Scofield Reference Bible*, ed. C. I. Scofield (NY: Oxford University Press, 1909), 1270. Jewett (*Paul's Anthropological Terms*, 175-183) argued that such trichotomy was an attempt to counteract Greek Gnosticism. However, Charles Wanamaker observed, "...we have no evidence for a developed Gnostic anthropology this early...if Paul had faced the difficulty [of dealing with this Greek viewpoint] it seems doubtful that a wish-prayer [1 Thes 5:23] was either an appropriate or adequate place to attempt to correct such a problem."—*Commentary on 1 Thessalonians* (Grand Rapids: Eerdmans:1990), 206.

[5] G. H. Pember, *Earth's Earliest Ages* (Grand Rapids: Kregel Publications, 1942), 77.

[6] Mark Cambron, *Bible Doctrine* (Grand Rapids: Zondervan, 1954), 158.

[7] Lewis S. Chafer, *Systematic Theology* (Dallas, TX: Dallas Seminary Press, 1947), 2:181.

[8] Ibid.

[9] Henry C. Thiessen, *Lectures in Systematic Theology* (Grand Rapids: Eerdmans, 1949), 227. James Fowler presents a functional trichotomy while opting to refrain from identifying "parts" of man. Yet, his article shows the problems inherent in monist and dichotomist models: "...God, as Trinitarian relational Spirit, created mankind with spiritual, psychological, and physiological function. Man is, therefore, capable of participating in a 'one spirit' (1 Cor. 6:17) union with God the Father, Son, and Holy Spirit..." James A. Fowler, *Toward A Christian Understanding Of Man* (www.ChristinYou.net, 2002) 3.

[10] Buswell, *A Systematic Theology of the Christian Religion*, 1:247.

[11] Franz Delitzsch, *A System of Biblical Psychology*, 99.

[12] Ibid.

[13] Ibid., 109.

[14] Ibid., 116.

[15] Ibid., 115-16.

[16] Ibid., 117.

[17] J. B. Heard, *The Tripartite Nature of Man*, 104.

[18] Clarence A. Beckwith, *Biblical Conceptions of Soul and Spirit* in *The New Schaff-Herzog Encyclopedia of Religious Knowledge*, ed. Samuel M. Jackson (NY: Funk and Wagnalls, 1911), 11:12.

[19] L. Thomas Holdcroft, *Anthropology: A Biblical View*, 23-24.

[20] Oswald Chambers, *Biblical Psychology*, 2d ed. (Grand Rapids: Discovery House, 1995), 46.

[21] Ibid., 210.

[22] Ibid., 33.

[23] Watchman Nee, *The Spiritual Man*, (NY: Christian Fellowship Publishers, 1968), 2:8.

[24] *The Scofield Reference Bible*, 1270.

[25] T. Austin Sparks, *What is Man?* (Cloverdale, IN: Ministry of Life, n. d.), 38.

[26] J. B. Heard, *The Tripartite Nature of Man*, 351.

[27] Jessie Penn-Lewis, *Soul and Spirit* (Fort Washington, PA: Christian Literature Crusade, 1992), 13.

[28] Kenneth Liu, *A Study of the Human Soul and Spirit*, unpublished thesis for Talbot Theological Seminary, 1966, 58; quoted in Holdcroft, *Anthropology: A Biblical View*, 25. Cf. Pember, *Earth's Earliest Ages*, 75.

[29] For a trichotomistic model that uses "heart" rather than a human "spirit," see Neil T. Anderson and Robert L. Saucy, *The Common Made Holy* (Eugene, OR: Harvest House, 1997), 79-100, 156.

[30] L. Thomas Holdcroft, *Anthropology: A Biblical View*, 21.

Man As Spirit, Soul, and Body

Chapter 3
Biblical Word Studies

The Role of Word Studies

Some scholars have been emphatic about the limitations of the Bible as a source book for a system of biblical psychology. An example of this reluctance is the analysis of G. C. Berkouwer, as translated by Anthony Hoekema:

> The general judgment [of theologians] is that the Bible gives us no scientific teaching about man, no "anthropology" that would or could be in competition with a scientific investigation of man in the various aspects of his existence or with philosophical anthropology.[1]

Others point out that the Scriptures do not use scientific language; essential words about man's makeup are used somewhat interchangeably. While sharing this reluctance to define a formal system of biblical psychology, conservative scholars acknowledge that the Bible's teaching is authoritative in clarifying every topic, including this one. Although the Bible does not purport to be a science textbook, the nature of verbal plenary inspiration requires the believing scholar to accept its teaching as authoritative. The scope of this authority reaches every area the Bible speaks to, including both seen and unseen realms. As J. I. Marais put it, "A reverent study of Scripture will undoubtedly lead to a well-defined system of psychology [the study of the immaterial part of man], on which the whole scheme of redemption is based."[2]

In the process of investigating scriptural teaching on topics such as the makeup of human beings, the discipline of biblical word studies is foundational. William Barclay declared:

> The more I study words, the more I am convinced of their basic and fundamental importance. On the meaning of words everything depends. No one can build up a theology [or psychology] without a clear definition of the terms which are to be used in it...Christian belief and Christian action both depend upon a clear understanding of the meaning of words. [3]

This study of essential vocabulary will depend upon the material in Hebrew and Greek lexicons and concordances. Etymology of ancient words is helpful, but usage is just as important in determining accurate definitions.

Terms Used for the Spirit

The word typically translated "spirit" in the Old Testament is *ruach*, which occurs about 380 times. (Note: A list of Hebrew and Greek vocabulary with definitions is listed in appendix A.) *Ruach* is probably related to the root meaning "to breathe." Its basic meanings include "wind," "breath," "mind," and "spirit." It is the noun of the Hebrew verb *riah*, meaning "to smell," "accept." In its concrete usage, *ruach* signifies the breath of living creatures (Job 15:50; 16:3), and is so used of people and rarely of animals (Isa 42:5; Ps 104:25,29).

As hard breathing in the nostrils, *ruach* is used figuratively to denote emotions such as anger in man or in God (Isa 25:4; Ex 15:8). This kind of quick breathing can convey various other dispositions of the inner self: vigor (1 Sam 30:12), courage (Josh 5:1), impatience (Micah 2:7), bitterness (Isa 54:6), jealousy (Hos 4:12), and motivation (Ezra 1:1,5). When the Queen of Sheba was overwhelmed by Solomon's attainments, she had no more *ruach*, i.e., was "breathless" (1 Kgs 10:5). A person's *ruach* may be contrite (Isa 57:15), or sad (1 Kgs 21:5). Spirit can likewise refer to one's character such as being wise (Deut 34:9), unfaithful (Hos 4:12), proud (Eccl 7:8), or jealous (Num 5:14).

In its use as atmospheric wind, *ruach* describes storm winds (Isa 25:4), directional winds, the four winds (Ex 10:13; Prov 25:23; Jer 49:36), or wind from heaven (Gen 8:1). Metaphorically, *ruach* can mean something vain or empty: "Remember that my life is a breath [*ruach*]! My eye will never again see good" (Job 7:7). This derivation of wind makes *ruach* more abstract from man than the basic idea of *nephesh* [soul] which was originally associated with the throat.

One of the main uses of ruach is to describe God. J. Barton Payne summarizes Old Testament references to the activity of the Spirit of God:

> The work of God's Spirit may be cosmic, whether in creation (Job 26:13) or in continuing providence (Job 33:4; Ps 104:30); redemptive, in regeneration (Ezek 11:19; 36:26,27); indwelling, to uphold and guide the believer (Neh 9:20; Ps 143:10; Hag 2:5); or infilling, for leadership (Num 11:25; Jud 6:34; 1 Sam 16:13), service (Num 11:17; Mic 3:8; Zech 7:12), or future empowering of the Messiah (Is 11:2; 42:1; 61:1), and his people (Joel 2:28; Is 32:15).[4]

These activities and attributes show that God's Spirit is more than an impersonal influence; He is a person. This doctrine of the Holy Spirit as a co-equal, distinct person of the Godhead is made explicit in the New Testament. Since the same Hebrew word for spirit is used in referring to God and man, the context is important in determining the exact usage. The same range of meaning occurs in the New Testament's use of *pneuma* [spirit]. Angels are other personal spiritual beings identified by *ruach* (1 Sam 16:23; Zech 1:9).

Although liberal scholars interpret ruach as an impersonal life-principle that cannot exist apart from the body, the Old Testament data support the essential dual nature of man as having distinct material and immaterial parts. Ecclesiastes 12:7 describes the outcome of man's physical death: "Then the dust will return to the earth as it was, And the spirit [*ruach*] will return to God who gave it." Both *nephesh* and *ruach* are said to leave the body at death and exist separately from it (Gen 35:18; Ps 86:13). The Hebrew emphasis on wholeness does not negate these observations.

This term *pneuma* is the New Testament equivalent of *ruach.* Occurring over 350 times, its essential definition is "wind," or "spirit." The root *pneu* has the idea of the dynamic movement of air. The related words convey the ideas of blowing (of the wind, or playing a musical instrument), breathing, emitting a fragrance, giving off heat, etc.[5] The verb form is always used of blowing wind in the New Testament (Matt 7:25,27), unless John 3:8 is interpreted as referring to the Holy Spirit's activity.

Although the noun *pneuma* can retain the literal idea of wind (Heb 1:7), it usually refers to spiritual beings, entities, or qualities. As the Old Testament usage of *nephesh* and *ruach* overlap, so also does the use of *psuche* and *pneuma*. F. Foulkes observed, "Many things can be said to describe the action of man's spirit as his functioning in his essential being."[6] In an abstract sense, *pneuma* can refer to one's purpose (2 Cor 12:18; Phil 1:27) or character (Luke 1:17; Rom 1:4). Moral qualities are spoken of in terms of spirit. Bad qualities include a spirit of bondage (Rom 8:15), stupor (Rom 11:8), or timidity (2 Tim 1:7); good qualities of spirit include faith (2 Cor 4:13), meekness (1 Cor 4:21), liberty (Rom 8:15), and quietness (1 Pet 3:4). Contextual clues are needed to determine when spirit is used in this abstract way.

Pneuma frequently refers to noncorporeal beings such as angels. Good angels are identified in passages such as Hebrews 1:14: "Are they not all ministering spirits sent forth to minister for those who will inherit salvation?" Bad angels are called unclean or evil spirits. Forty times the New Testament mentions this class of fallen angels as "spirits" (e.g., Matt 8:16; Luke 4:33). Since the spirit of man can be influenced by good or evil spiritual beings, believers are summoned to exercise discernment: "Beloved, do not believe every spirit, but test the spirits, whether they are of God..." (1 John 4:1). This conflict of good versus evil should not be construed as teaching the Greek conception of dualism. As Colin Brown notes,

> But at no time do the N. T. writers give way to dualism, where the evil which thus manifests itself is as strong as God. Always the evil spirits are shown inferior to God and subject to the power of the Spirit of God operating through his agents.[7]

Thus, God's sovereignty is not compromised.

Pneuma is also used of the third person of the triune God, Who is co-equal and co-eternal with the Father and the Son. He is designated by *pneuma* about ninety times in the New Testament. Sometimes the definite article is used which is common when the context emphasizes His personality, or His distinction from the Father and the Son (Matt 12:31,32; John 14:26; 15:26).[8] In some contexts the distinction between man's spirit and the Holy Spirit is ambiguous. For example, Romans 8:4,5 states:

> That the righteous requirement of the law might be fulfilled in us who do not walk according to the flesh but according to the Spirit [or spirit]. For those who live according to the flesh set their minds on the things of the flesh, but those who live according to the Spirit [or spirit], the things of the Spirit.

The regenerating work of the Spirit of God in the believer makes man's spirit alive, but He does not take the place of it. As Cremer's lexicon observed:

> Always according to the context, we must understand by *pneuma* the divine life-principle by nature peculiar to man, either in its natural position within his organism [the creation of Adam], or as renewed by the communication of the Spirit [at salvation]...But we must hold fast the truth, that this newly given life-principle [the Spirit in His regenerating work—Rom 8:9] does not become identical with the spirit belonging to man by nature, nor does it supplant it.[9]

Pneuma refers to a part of man's makeup about forty times. This does not endorse the Greek model of trichotomy that equates spirit with reason and views matter as evil.

> The N. T. writers can speak of the human spirit as though it was a something possessed by the individual; but this does not mean they envisaged the spirit of man as a divine spark (the real 'I') incarcerated in the physical.[10]

The *pneuma* in man is not a universal spirit or perfected soul. When contrasted with flesh, *pneuma* refers to man's immaterial part (2 Cor 7:1). Like the soul, it can refer to man as temporarily separated from his physical body; thus Hebrews 12:23 can speak of the scene of God's presence in heaven as accompanied by "the spirits of just men made perfect" (cf. Luke 24:37,39).

The usage of *pneuma* often overlaps that of *psuche*, but some passages indicate that they are more than synonyms for the immaterial part of man. An analysis of their New Testament usage shows distinctive connotations for each of them.[11]   In 1 Thessalonians 5:22,23 and Hebrews 4:12, they do not merely refer to different functions or roles; they are identified as distinct parts of man.

The use of the adjective *pneumatikos* and adverb *pneumatikoos* further substantiate the distinction between soul and spirit. Thayer gives one of the definitions of the adjective *pneumatikos* "as the part of man which is akin to God and serves as his instrument or organ" (cf. 1 Cor 15:44,46).[12] The adverb *pneumatikoos* seems to allude to the *pneuma* as a distinct part of man in 1 Corinthians 2:14:

> But the natural [soulical] man does not receive the things of the Spirit of God, for they are foolishness to him; nor can he know them, because they are spiritually [relating to the spirit] discerned.

Terms Used for the Soul

The Hebrew term for soul is *nephesh*, occurring about 750 times in the Old Testament. The root idea of *nephesh* and related cognate words in Akkadian and Ugaritic is "throat," or "breath." Brown, Driver, and Briggs' lexicon classifies ten shades of meaning for this word, including "soul," "life," "creature," "person," and "mind."[13] *Nephesh* identifies that which breathes. It can be distinct from the body (Isa 10:8), yet is closely associated with it (Job 14:23). *Nephesh* leaves the man's body at death, and if it returns supernaturally, the body's life is restored (1 Kgs 17:21; Gen 35:18).

Living creatures exist due to the creative acts of God. Animals were created and designated as having *nephesh* (Gen 2:19,30). (Man's creation was distinct from animals by virtue of his higher status; he was made in the image of God—Gen 1:26; 2:7.) Life is identified with a creature's blood; this forms the basis of the value of substitutionary sacrifice of animals. In Leviticus 17:11 God states,

> For the life [*nephesh*] of the flesh is in the blood, and I have given it to you upon the altar to make atonement for your

souls [*nephesh*]; for it is the blood that makes atonement for the soul [*nephesh*].

In the first occurrence, *nephesh* refers to "vitality, the passionate existence of an individual."[14] However, the latter two occurrences ("your soul") seem to point to the person's spiritual life.

Since *nephesh* conveys the idea of individual life, it can stand for the man himself (without distinguishing his immaterial side). It identifies people in the poetic literature (Ps 25:12), as well as the historical literature (Num 30:14). It is used in numbering people (Josh 10:28), and can refer to individuals or groups (Deut 4:9: Isa 46:2). By a peculiar figure of speech, *nephesh* is used of dead bodies in Numbers 5:2; 6:6. How can the noun indicating "breath" be used of a body not breathing? Waltke explains that when *nephesh* is applied to a dead person, it is used to emphasize their identity as persons who have died, not to equate *nephesh* with the body.[15]

The other uses of the term cover areas related to man's appetites, will, emotions, and thoughts. *Nephesh* can indicate man's appetites such as hunger (Deut 23:24), thirst (Ps 107:9), and the sexual drive (Jer 2:24). Man's soul can express volition toward an enemy (Ex 15:9), or extending political rule (2 Sam 3:21). The soul's capacity to love is mentioned in Song of Solomon 1:7; 3:1-4. *Nephesh* can extend love in friendship (1 Sam 20:17), or its opposite—hatred (2 Sam 5:8). The soul can express a variety of emotions, such as joy or sorrow (Ps 86:4; Job 27:2) and personal thoughts (Prov 23:17).

Rarely, *nephesh* is used of God. This differs from the usual meanings and should be understood in a figurative sense because "God does not have the cravings and appetites common to man nor is his life limited by death."[16] God rebuked Judah, "'Shall I not punish them for these things?' says the LORD. And shall I not avenge Myself [my *nephesh*] on such a nation as this?'" (Jer 5:9). This example shows the reason for the use of *nephesh*. In this context the connotation of hard breathing expresses the intensity of God's holy zeal. Since it conveys the idea of breathing, *nephesh* is usually associated with the physical nature of man. However, this emphasis in Hebrew thought must not ignore the texts cited above which indicate that the soul is distinct and separable from the body.

This distinctive aspect of soul becomes more pronounced in the equivalent term in the New Testament, *psuche.* This word for soul occurs about 100 times in the New Testament. It is derived from the verb *psucho,* "to breathe." *Psuche* occurs about 600 times in the LXX (the Greek translation of the Hebrew Old Testament) as the translation of *nephesh.* Cremer's lexicon gives its basic meaning:

> In universal usage, from Homer downwards, *psuche* signifies life in the distinctiveness of individual existence, especially of man, and occasionally, but only *ex analogia,* of brutes...As to the use of the word in Scripture, first in the O. T. it corresponds with *nephesh,* primarily likewise—life, breath, the life which exists in every living thing, therefore life in distinct individuality.[17]

In classical Greek, *psuche* originally had an impersonal connotation; *thumos* was more apt to refer to the conscious soul. Eventually, the meaning of *psuche* broadened to include both life and consciousness, which is expressed in the Koine Greek of the New Testament.[18]

The basic usage of *psuche* conveys the idea of "the vital force which animates the body and shows itself in breathing."[19] It is used in that sense regarding people (Acts 20:10) and animals (Rev 8:9). This natural life of the body is used to affirm the humanity Christ (Matt 2:20). In His ministry Jesus counseled, "Therefore I say to you, do not worry about your life [*psuche*], what you will eat; nor about the body, what you will put on" (Luke 12:22). In sacrificial love, Jesus laid down his life [*psuche*] for His sheep (John 10:11). Since the soul animates the body, these two aspects of man are interrelated. By synecdoche [a figure of speech by which a part is put for the whole], soul can be used to denote the person or organism which has life (1 Cor 15:45); "every soul" can mean "every one" (Acts 2:43; 3:23). Likewise, in enumeration, people can be identified as "souls" (Acts 2:41).

Another meaning of *psuche* is to denote man's inner self. The inner functions of soul include emotions such as sorrow (Matt 26:38), discouragement (Heb 12:3), vexation (2 Pet 2:8), joy (Luke 1:46), zeal (Col 3:23), and love (Matt 22:37). The will and desire are also functions of the soul (Eph 6:6; Rev 18:14). These responses necessarily involve perception (Acts 3:23; Heb 4:12).

These faculties describe the individual's personality. "*Psuche* means the inner life of man, equivalent to the ego, person, or personality, with the various powers of the soul."[20]   Paul and his co-workers lovingly imparted, as it were, their very souls to the Thessalonian church (1 Thes 2:8). Christ offered peace and rest of soul to those who come to Him (Matt 11:29).

An important issue for this study on the constituent parts of man is the question: Is the *psuche* an immaterial, invisible part of man, or simply an aspect of the living, physical body? While not retaining the Greek idea of the innate immortality of the soul, the New Testament usage indicates that the soul is a distinct and separable part of man: "And do not fear those who kill the body but cannot kill the soul..." (Matt 10:28). This soul is the "essence which differs from the body and is not dissolved at death."[21]   Salvation involves saving the soul unto eternal life (Heb 10:38; 1 Pet 1:3-9).

> James 1:21 and 5:20 speak of the salvation of the soul which is in danger. The death from which it is said that the soul will be saved is eternal death, exclusion from eternal life... The soul, is the part of us which believes, is sanctified, and is destined to an inheritance in God's future kingdom. [22]

This salvation requires purification by God's grace (1 Pet 1:22). Spiritual life has greater value than mere physical life, for it continues after death (John 12:25; Phil 1:23).

The soul is identified as a distinct part of man when it is contrasted to the physical part: "Beloved, I pray that you may prosper in all things and be in health, just as your soul prospers" (3 John 2). Although the concept of this separation of the soul from the body is found in Greek literature, in the writings of Josephus, and in Philo of Alexandria, the biblical doctrine is based on exegesis of the text of the New Testament.[23] The intermediate state of the believer between death and resurrection involves the conscious soul:

> I saw under the altar the souls of those who had been slain for the word of God and for the testimony which they held. And they cried with a loud voice, saying, "How long, O Lord, holy and true, until You judge and avenge our blood on those who dwell on the earth?" (Rev 6:9,10; cf. 20:4).

Although this quotation comes from apocalyptic literature, the intermediate state is also evident in historical passages. On the Mount of Transfiguration Jesus spoke with Moses and Elijah after their physical death (Matt 17:3).

Terms Used for the Body

The primary word for the physical body of living things in the Old Testament is *basar.* It occurs over 250 times in the Hebrew Bible almost always translated "flesh." *Basar* is used of the body of man corporately and individually (Deut 5:26; Num 8:7). When God created Eve, he used part of Adam's "flesh" (Gen 2:21), and their sexual relationship was described as being "one flesh." *Basar* sometimes refers to kindred relationships, as when Joseph's brothers decided not to kill him since he was their brother, i.e. their "flesh" (Gen 37:27). In Genesis 6:3 God announced "My Spirit shall not strive with man forever, for he is indeed flesh; yet his days shall be one hundred and twenty years." Such contexts imply mankind as frail, having a tendency to stray from God (Gen 6:12). The Psalmist contrasted the limitations of man's attacks (his enemy's flesh) with the sufficiency of God's strength (Ps 56:4).

The fleshly body was sometimes differentiated from man's mortal life. Job anticipated his bodily resurrection: "And after my skin is destroyed, this I know, That *in my flesh* I shall see God" (Job 19:26). God contrasts His nature with that of ba-sar in Isaiah 31:33: "Now the Egyptians are men, and not God; And their horses are *flesh*, and not spirit..." In Numbers 16:22, the LORD is called "the God of the spirits of all *flesh.*" The physical body of man is often referred to in the Old Testament, yet without limiting him to a material nature. Additional terms used less frequently in the Old Testament could be mentioned, but since there are about eighty different Hebrew terms for the body and its members, the above word study will suffice.

The most basic term in the New Testament for the body is *soma*, which occurs some 146 times. *Soma* can also be used of plant, animal, or celestial "bodies" (Heb 13:11; 1 Cor 15:37, 40). Metaphorically, it can describe the spiritual union of true believers as "the body" of Christ (Rom 12:5). It is also used of the elements of the bread and wine in the Lord's Supper, when Christ called them "My body" (Matt 26:26).

Man As Spirit, Soul, and Body

The use of *soma* for man's body avoids Greek notions of the innate inferiority of matter. As B. O. Banwell observed,

> The New Testament usage of soma, "body," comes close to the Hebrew and avoids the thought of Greek philosophy, which tends to castigate the body as evil, the prison of the soul or reason, which was seen as good.[24]

For example, "the Lord is for the body" (1 Cor 6:13); husbands are expected to love their wives as their own bodies (Eph 5:28), and food should be given to satisfy the hunger of the body (Jas 2:16). Evil comes from the heart, not just from bodily appetites (Luke 6:45). Nevertheless, the freedom of man's will, the pressures of a sinful society, demonic influence, and the flesh conspire to make the mortal body of fallen man a source of continual vulnerability and temptation (Rom 6:12). The way to godliness requires self-discipline but not asceticism (1 Cor 9:27; Col 2:23). Physical pleasure within the boundaries of God's design are credited as His gifts (1 Cor 7:14; 1 Tim 6:17). The body of the believer in Christ has special dignity as the temple of the Holy Spirit (1 Cor 6:19).

The use of *soma* indicates that the body is an integral part of man, yet distinct from his immaterial element. In Revelation 18:13 body and soul together describe man. Jesus affirmed the contrast of these two elements in Matthew 10:28: "And do not fear those who kill the body but cannot kill the soul. But rather fear Him who is able to destroy both soul and body in hell." In 2 Corinthians 12:2,3, Paul distinguished these elements of man as separable and distinct:

> I know a man in Christ who fourteen years ago—whether in the body I do not know, or whether out of the body I do not know, God knows—such a one was caught up to the third heaven. And I know such a man—whether in the body or out of the body I do not know, God knows.

James notes that faith without works is dead even as the physical body without the spirit is dead (Jas 2:26).

The other major word used in the New Testament to describe the human body is *sarx.* Appearing about 150 times in the text, its primary meaning is "flesh"; approximating the meaning of the Hebrew word *basar.* It is used to denote the flesh of animals and man (1 Cor 15:39). *Sarx* can be ethically neutral, referring to man's material nature, or of social status (1 Cor 1:26; Eph 6:5). It is also used to denote heredity (Rom 9:3), Christ's incarnation (1 Tim 3:16; Heb 5:7), and the believer's life in the body (Gal 2:20). As a part of man, it is sometimes used to represent the whole of him (Acts 2:17). *Sarx* is sometimes used to distinguish man's material body from his immaterial self. When Jesus evangelized Nicodemus, He emphasized the imperative of the new birth: "That which is born of the *flesh* is *flesh*, and that which is born of the Spirit is spirit" (John 3:6). Christ further contrasted flesh and spirit in describing the nature of His redeeming work: "It is the Spirit who gives life; the *flesh* profits nothing. The words that I speak to you are spirit, and they are life" (John 6:63).

The New Testament further specifies the natural state of those unregenerated as "in the flesh" (Rom 7:5), who characteristically "walk after the *flesh*" (2 Pet 2:10). Those who are redeemed by Christ are not exempt from the ongoing effects of the flesh as a negative influence. The ethical use of *sarx* is typically evil, indicating selfish autonomy instead of godliness. Paul uses *sarx* this way in Romans 7:18: "For I know that in me (that is, in my flesh) nothing good dwells..."

The Heart: Not a Fourth Part

The Old Testament uses *leb* for heart, which was usually translated as *kardia* in the LXX. The Hebrew use of heart was either physical (Gen 18:5; Jud 19:5) or metaphorical. The latter use is the common one, which viewed the heart as the seat of man's spiritual and intellectual life. This involved the emotions (Deut 28:47), the mind (1 Kgs 3:12; 4:29), and the will (Ex 36:2). *Leb* is,

> ...a comprehensive term for the personality as a whole, its inner life, its character. It is the conscious and deliberate spiritual activity of the self-contained human ego and the seat of his responsibility.[25]

The New Testament term for "heart" is *kardia*, which occurs almost 150 times. The use of *kardia* in the New Testament is consistent with *leb*. It rarely refers to the physical heart (Luke 21:34), but characteristically describes the inner life of man (2 Cor 5:12). This use of *kardia* can represent the whole inner life (1 Pet 3:4), the psychological part of man (2 Cor 4:6; 9:7; Eph 6:22), or his spiritual orientation (Matt 22:37). The sinful heart is deceitful (Mark 7:6), enslaved (Mark 7:21), and corrupt (Rom 1:24). Through salvation in Christ the heart is opened to God's grace (Acts 16:4), illumined by His truth (2 Cor 4:6), and enriched by His love (Rom 5:5). *There is not adequate biblical evidence for identifying heart as a fourth constituent part of man, distinct from soul and spirit.* The believer's new heart is explored further in appendix E.

Other related terms in the New Testament express different aspects of man's inner life. The "mind" is translated from *phronema* and usually occurs in its verbal form (Acts 28:22; Rom 12:3). The "will" is translated from the verbs *thelo* (Matt 1:19;8:2), or *boulomai* (Luke 10:22; John 18:39); and emotions are described by a variety of nouns and verbs. The spiritual function of conscience is denoted by *suneidesis* (Acts 23:1). Inductive word studies lead to the conclusion that such terms identify various functional attributes of the soul and spirit.

Summary

The word studies in this chapter have traced the meaning and usage of the basic terms in the Bible that relate to man's makeup. This data show many ways that soul and spirit are used interchangeably, especially in the Old Testament. Some distinctions in New Testament usage between soul and spirit have been noted and more will be identified in subsequent chapters. Milton Terry resisted coming to a conclusion about the doctrine of man's makeup based only on "the rhetorical language of biblical writers who follow no uniform usage of the same words."[26] However, he and other dichotomists uniformly agree that spirit has a higher connotation than soul in biblical literature. While it is conceded that word studies alone are not conclusive for this doctrinal issue, biblical exposition gives adequate evidence to support the distinction of soul and spirit as being more than merely one of emphasis. McClintock and Strong's encyclopedia concluded that distinctions in biblical vocabulary usage for spirit, soul, and body were substantial enough to support the tripartite makeup of man.[27] This issue is relevant because a precise theological model of man's constituent parts and their faculties is integral to one's view of sanctification, psychology, and counseling. The next chapter will build on this foundation of word studies by surveying the key aspects of redemption history, seeking to highlight the significance it has on the makeup of man.

[1] Anthony A. Hoekema, *Created in God's Image* (Grand Rapids: Eerdmans, 1986), 203.

[2] James Orr, ed., *The International Standard Bible Encyclopedia*, s.v. "Psychology," by J. I. Marais, 4:2495.

[3] William Barclay, *More New Testament Words* (New York: Harper, 1958), 9. Quoted in Cyril J. Barber, *Introduction to Theological Research* (Chicago: Moody Press, 1982), 111.

[4] J. Barton Payne, TWBOT, 2:837.

[5] Colin Brown ed., *The New International Dictionary of New Testament Theology*, [NIDNTT] (Exeter: Paternoster Press, 1975), s.v. "Spirit," 3: 689.

[6] M. Tenney ed., *The Zondervan Pictorial Encyclopedia of the Bible* [ZPEB], s.v. "Spirit" by F. Foulkes, 5:505.

[7] Brown, NIDNTT, 695.

[8] W. E. Vine, *Expository Dictionary of New Testament Words*, (Westood, NJ: Flemming H. Revell, 1940), 63.

[9] Cremer, BTLNTG, 506.

[10] Brown, NIDNTT, 3: 694.

[11] Thayer, GELNT, 523.

[12] Brown, NIDNTT, 2:181.

[13] F. Brown, S. R. Driver, and C. A. Briggs ed., *Hebrew and English Lexicon to the Old Testament* (Oxford: Oxford University Press, 1957), s.v. "Nephesh," 659.

[14] Laird Harris, Gleason Archer, and Bruce Waltke eds., *The Theological Wordbook of the Old Testament* [TWBOT], s.v. "Nephesh," by Bruce Waltke, 2:590.

[15] Ibid.

[16] Ibid., 591.

[17] Herman Cremer, *Biblical-Theological Lexicon of the New Testament Greek,* [BTLNTG] trans. William Urwick (Edinburgh: T. & T. Clark, 1895), s.v. "Psuche," 592,93.

[18] Colin Brown ed., *The New International Dictionary of New Testament Theology,* [NIDNTT] (Exeter: Paternoster Press, 1975), s.v. "Soul," 3: 677.

[19] Joseph H.Thayer, *A Greek-English Lexicon of the New Testament* [GELNT] (Grand Rapids: Baker Book House, 1977), s.v. "Psuche," 677.

[20] Brown, NIDNTT, 3: 683.

[21] Thayer, GELNT, 677.

[22] Brown, NIDNTT, 3: 685.

[23] Brown, IDNTT, 3: 681.

[24] J. D. Douglas, *New Bible Dictionary* (Wheaton: Tyndale House, 1962), s.v. "Body," by B. O. Banwell, 145.

[25] R. W. F. Wooton, *Spirit and Soul in the New Testament,* The Bible Translator, 26 (1975) 239-44.

[26] Milton S. Terry, *Biblical Dogmatics: An Exposition of the Principal Doctrines of the Holy Scriptures* (NY: Eaton and Mains, 1907), 53.

[27] John McClintock and John Strong, *Cyclopedia of Biblical, Theological, and Ecclesiastical Literature,* s.v. "Soul," 9:891. Harold Willmington gives a review of the cases for dichotomy and trichotomy, then nods to the conclusion of *Unger's Bible Dictionary,* p. 1043: "The two terms [soul and spirit] are often used interchangeably... however, soul and spirit as synonymous terms are not always employed interchangeably. The soul is said to be lost, for example, but not the spirit. When no technical distinctions are set forth, the Bible is dichotomous, but otherwise it is trichotomous..." *Introduction to Theology,* 261.

Chapter 4
Trichotomy in Redemptive History

The Context of Biblical Redemption

This study of redemptive history examines the major biblical and theological stages in the sequence of salvation and their implications on the human spirit, soul, and body. This chapter will include the exegesis of relevant passages that relate to the issue of man's makeup. The basic stages identified below include creation, the Fall, the new birth, sanctification, physical death, and bodily resurrection.

The principle of *progressive revelation* will be germane to the interpretation of biblical passages examined. Heard noted the importance of understanding this concept:

> It would be out of harmony with the "analogy of faith" if the tripartite nature of man were fully described in those [more ancient] books of the Bible which only contain implied hints of the plurality of the Godhead. All we shall see of the subject will confirm this view of the harmonious way in which doctrines and duties, the nature of God, and the nature of man, are unfolded together.[1]

In the Bampton Lectures at Oxford, Thomas Bernard confirmed this understanding, clarifying that progressive revelation terminated at the completion of the Bible:

> In speaking, therefore, of the progress of doctrine in the New Testament, I speak of a course of communication from God which reaches its completion within those limits, constituting a perfected scheme of divine teaching, open to new elucidations and deductions, but not to the addition of new materials.[2]

Biblical theology unfolds with increasing detail and scope from the earliest writings in the Bible to its conclusion. The study of man's makeup, especially his immaterial aspects, requires careful consideration of this principle of progressive revelation.

Creation

The Bible affirms man's unique status in creation as made in God's image (Gen 1:26,27). The theological implications of this truth are many and varied. Some have argued for trichotomy as a reflection of God's triune nature. It has been noted that the noun used for "God" (*Elohim*) is in the plural (three or more) form, yet takes a singular verb form ("Let us [plural] create [singular]"). This fits what later revelation shows to be God's triune nature. Since man is made in God's image, is the Trinity a proof of man's three-in-one nature as spirit, soul, and body? Some find this to be compelling evidence. In his book on Christian counseling, Ed Bulkley sees the role of man's creation in the image of the triune God as a deciding factor in seeing the soul and spirit as distinct from each other:

> My support for trichotomy is based on a different foundation entirely [than proof texts]—the Trinity. God has given us many illustrations of the Trinity in our universe: time (past, present, and future), three dimensions (length, width, and height), the three states of water (liquid, gas, and solid), and so on... Genesis 1:27 says that "God made man in his own image, in the image of God created he him." Let me explain why it is possible for that image to be triune, consisting of the material (the physical body), life itself (called "the breath of life" or the spirit), and the soul (spoken of as heart, soul, or mind).[3]

Bulkley proceeds to observe three levels of life: plants (material), animals (more complex, having breath and conscious life), and man. God's image in man, therefore, would involve the human spirit which is in addition to material substance and animal life. Therefore, God's triune nature is a confirming evidence, even if not a "proof," of man's trichotomy.

The creation text that most directly relates to the issue of man's makeup is Genesis 2:7: "And the LORD God formed man of the dust of the ground, and breathed into his nostrils

Man As Spirit, Soul, and Body

the breath of life; and man became a living being." The material used in man's creation was the dust of the ground. The Hebrew term for "ground" here, *adamah*, is related to the name given to the first man—Adam. The phrase "breath of life" is literally breath of "lives" [*hayim*]. This use of the plural form may imply a distinction of soul and spirit.

Genesis 2:7 reveals the dignity of man; his creation was distinct from the method of creating other living creatures. As Delitzsch put it, "The spirit of man is an immediate inspiration of God, the personal transmitted into the bodily form..."[4] Man became a living "soul" [*nephesh*], which by synecdoche represents the whole living person. The creation of a distinct spirit in man is consistent with God's nature as a spirit (John 4:24) and Paul's endorsement of the quotation, "we are His offspring" (Acts 17:28). God is also called "the Father of our spirits" (Heb 12:9). Although the first man was directly created by God from dust through the breath of God's Spirit, Genesis does not reveal the way Adam's descendants would acquire their immaterial side. Some theologians favor the view that the soul is directly created by God for each child (creationism) others, that it is passed on through the parents (traducianism).

McClintock and Strong's comprehensive encyclopedia refers to Genesis 2:7 as relevant to the issue of man's makeup:

> The passage of Scripture which is fundamental in this inquiry [of the soul/spirit distinction] (Gen. 2:7) seems, however, to distinguish three constituents in human nature— *the clay, the breath of life, and the living being*...Scripture teaches a trichotomy and several passages explicitly sustain this same doctrine—e.g., Luke 1:46,47; 1 Cor. 15:45ff; 1 Thes 5:23; Heb 4:12.[5]

Thus, the creation of man in God's image and the threefold aspect of the creation account of Genesis 2:7 point to man's triunity.

The Fall

Adam's fall into sin had devastating effects on the human race. In Genesis 2:16,17 God warned Adam about the consequences that would follow any violation of the divine law:

And the LORD God commanded the man, saying, "Of every tree of the garden you may freely eat; but of the tree of the knowledge of good and evil you shall not eat, for in the day that you eat of it you shall surely die."

No other created being on earth was given this moral test. The exercise of spiritual and moral volition corresponds to the faculty of conscience in man's spirit. The capacity for moral choice is one aspect of man's status as made in God's image.

In this test of obedience lay the real superiority of Adam over every other living creature. Thus the contingence of evil could have been avoided only in one way, i.e., by denying to man the spiritual part altogether. Freedom to choose the good and to refuse the evil is an essential faculty of the human spirit. When Adam and Eve violated God's solitary prohibition, they plunged the human race into sin, misery, and death. God pronounced His curse upon the serpent, the woman, the man, and the sphere of man's dominion—earth (Gen 3:14-19).

The examination of the parts of human makeup leads to this relevant question: In what way did man die at the Fall? If one takes the warning of God precisely, the body did not "die" on the day of Adam's transgression. (Even though "day" [*yom*] can be translated "period of time," there is no hint in the context of anything other than a literal twenty four hour day.) Although the body was rendered mortal and separated from potential access to the tree of life, Adam lived to the age of 930 (Gen 5:5), so his body did not die on the day of original sin. The Hebrew of God's warning in Genesis 2:17 is *moth tamuth* ("dying you shall die"). The emphatic grammar points to an immediate consequence on the day of Adam's sin, followed by related effects.

Since the body did not die on the day of man's fall, what part of him *did* die? The soul (identified primarily with the faculties of mind, will, and emotions) was affected by original sin, yet was still alive and functioning. This leads to the deduction that *man's spirit was the locus of the immediate "death" spoken of in Genesis 2:17.* Proverbs 20:27 states, "The spirit of a man is the lamp of the LORD, Searching all the inner depths of his heart." This lamp was darkened by the Fall. Since many references to man's spirit occur between the Fall and redemption, it should not be assumed that man's fallen spirit ceases to exist prior to regeneration.

Man As Spirit, Soul, and Body

Adam's spirit died (was separated from God) at the Fall. Each person born in Adam inherits this condition of spiritual death. Lehman Strauss described the Fall's impact this way:

> In his unfallen state the "spirit" of man was illumined from heaven, but when the human race fell in Adam, sin closed the window of the spirit, pulled down the curtain, and the chamber of the spirit became a death chamber and remains so in every unregenerate heart until the power of the Holy Spirit floods the chamber with the Life and Light giving power of the new life in Christ Jesus.[6]

Thus, the human spirit has a distinctive role in defining the consequences of Adam's fall on all of his descendants.

Wayne Grudem, in his arguments against trichotomy, implies that the spirit of an unbeliever is not specifically dead because it is mentioned in Scripture (Deut 2:30), and is still active (Ps 78:8).[7] Yet, death needs to be defined scripturally; it essentially denotes *separation.* For example, at death the soul *separates* from the body (2 Cor 5:7) and at the "second death" the unsaved are *separated* from God's heaven (Rev 20:14). Admittedly, because man is unified in personhood and his spiritual death affects every area of his life (total depravity). Yet this does not negate the conclusion that his spirit was the specific locus of death on the day of Adam's fall. Thus, spiritual death is a separation of man's spirit from the life of God. This effect of sin is documented in passages such as Isaiah 59:2: "But your iniquities have separated you from your God; And your sins have hidden His face from you..." (cf. Matt 8:22; Eph 2:1,5; Rev 3:1). Therefore, man's spirit—his faculty of communion with God—was cut off from its source of life, like a cut flower is severed from its roots. This consequence is summarized in Romans 5:12: "Therefore, just as through one man sin entered the world, and death through sin, and thus death spread to all men, because all sinned." Apart from Christ, man's spirit is dormant toward the life of God—"dead" (1 Tim 5:6).

The bonding between spirit and soul has distorted the soul's functions as well. Herbert Lockyer noted,

> Man's whole being is corrupted—his spirit is darkened (Eph 4:17,18; 1 Cor 2:14); his soul is debased (Jer 17:9; Eph 4:19); his body is diseased and death-ridden (Rom 7:24)...

Sin brought a schism into man's nature, the lower dominating the higher.[8]

Another effect of the Fall is the upsetting of the government of man's constitutional nature. As Adam was to take dominion over the created order, he was designed naturally to rule the appetites of his body. The spirit, as his organ of communion with God, was to express itself through the soul, and through the body. Spiritual death, however, subjected mankind to what Luther called "the bondage of the will."[9] A conflict between conscience and choice would be a common feature of humankind's experience as fallen beings (Gal 5:16; Rom 7:7-24). Regarding man's inner government, T. Austin-Sparks wrote,

> It was in the upsetting of this order that function was affected fatally, and man became other than God had intended him to be...Instead of allowing his spirit to bring God in [at the moment of original temptation] man acted independently... Then the spirit of man, being so seriously violated, ceased to be the link between himself and God. Fellowship with God, which is always spiritual, was destroyed and the spirit sank down into subjection to man's soul.[10]

These observations concerning the Fall confirm the value of distinguishing spirit from soul.

Regeneration

The Greek term for regeneration is *paliggenesia*, which is used to describe the new life the Holy Spirit gives to the believer at salvation.

> Not by works of righteousness which we have done, but according to His mercy He saved us, through the washing of *regeneration* and renewing of the Holy Spirit" (Tit 3:5).

This concept is usually conveyed by the verb *gennao* or *anagennao*—"to beget" or "to beget again" (John 1:13; 3:3-8; 1 Pet 1:23; 1 John 2:29; 4:7; 5:1,4,18). James 1:18 describes this act of birth by the verb *apokueo*—"to bear or bring forth." Berkhof defined it this way: "Regeneration is that act of God by which the principle of the new life is implanted in man, and the gov-

Man As Spirit, Soul, and Body

erning disposition of the soul is made holy."[11] The trichotomist believes that this governing disposition is resident in the part known as the *human spirit*.

Regeneration is that aspect of conversion whereby God reverses spiritual death and implants new life in the believer. This new life is "created" by God (Eph 2:10), and it results in the believer being a "new creation" (2 Cor 5:17; Gal 6:15). One's view of man's constituent parts affects the interpretation of the negative results of the Fall as well as the positive dynamic of the new birth. Dichotomists emphasize that regeneration affects the whole person. Scripture does affirm such positive benefits to the soul, including the faculties of mind (Col 3:10), the will (Phil 2:13), and the emotions (Matt 5:4; 1 Pet 1:8). However, these benefits do not rid the believer of the sin principle, especially the "flesh" (Rom 7:17,18).

Jude 13 warns against false teachers, identifying them as unsaved—awaiting the punishment of hell. These individuals are described as "...sensual persons, who cause divisions, not having the Spirit" (Jude 19). Since the original uncial Greek text did not differentiate upper from lower case, the decision on rendering *pneuma* "Spirit" (for the Spirit of God) or "spirit" (for the spirit of man) is an editorial one. The Greek text has *pneuma ma exontes* ("spirit not having"). The definite article is not used with *pneuma*, yet English translations usually render *pneuma* "Spirit," corroborating other texts which indicate that the Holy Spirit only indwells believers (Eph 1:13). This, however, does not rule out that Jude may have been describing these false teachers as not having a human spirit that was rightly functioning, i.e., made alive. It is significant that the word "sensual" in verse 19 is the adjective for soul—*psuchikoi.* Pember commented on the significance of this contrast:

> *psuchikoi pneuma ma exontes,* scarcely "the Spirit." The preceding *psuchikoi* [soulical] makes the contrast between the human soul and spirit so obvious and natural that, if Jude had meant the Holy Spirit, he would surely have guarded this meaning by prefixing the article to *pneuma.* However, it does not seem necessary to press the sense further to understand that, in the men described, the God-consciousness is stifled [removed] by sensuousness. Even in their case the spirit may still be a potentiality, though as regards present influence it is as good as dead.[12]

These false teachers are spiritually dead, like "...late autumn trees without fruit, twice dead, pulled up by the roots" (Jude 12).

The believer is spiritually alive through regeneration, yet his body is still mortal—subject to sickness, aging, and death. Its susceptibility to convey the temptations of the flesh and the world system earns it the title of "this body of death" (Rom 7:24). If regeneration's effects on the body are less pronounced than its effects on the soul, it is not unlikely that the soul is less affected at regeneration than the spirit. Since Scripture indicates that man's spirit is the locus of his communion with God (John 4:23,24; Phil 3:3), it logically follows that its "death" at the Fall would correspond to its being "made alive" at regeneration (Eph 2:1,5).

The source of this change is spiritual union with (but not assimilation by) the Holy Spirit. "But he who is joined to the Lord is one spirit with Him" (1 Cor 6:17). The Holy Spirit also gives subjective assurance of this reality: "The Spirit Himself bears witness with our spirit that we are children of God" (Rom 8:16). Christ is involved in this work as the "life-giving spirit" in contrast to Adam, a living soul (1 Cor 15:45).

Sanctification

1 Thessalonians 5:23 presents a clear picture of the three parts of man in relation to sanctification. Paul wrote, "Now may the God of peace Himself sanctify you completely; and may your whole *spirit, soul,* and *body* be preserved blameless at the coming of our Lord Jesus Christ."

Non-trichotomists draw attention to the concept of "entire," *oloklaros,* and dismiss the significance of the terms Paul used to describe man. This text, however, is one of most explicit ones in the New Testament epistles on the topic of biblical psychology. Jamieson, Fausset, and Brown's commentary notes the importance of these terms:

> All three, spirit, soul, and body, each in its due place, constitute man "entire." The "spirit" links man with the higher intelligences of heaven, and is that highest part of man which is receptive to the quickening Holy Spirit (1 Cor 15:47). In the unspiritual, the spirit is so sunk under the lower animal soul...that such are termed 'animal' (E. V.

"sensual, having merely the body of organized matter, and the soul the immaterial animating essence), not having the Spirit [Jude 13].[13]

The sequence of the spirit, soul, and body also seems significant. Heard noted,

> The order...spirit, soul, and body, seems to point to the work [of sanctification] being progressive, as well an entire work. The Divine Spirit enters and dwells in our spirits first. From thence he gets the mastery over the desires of the mind, and lastly over the desires of the flesh.[14]

In his exposition of this passage, John Lineberry presents a concise trichotomous interpretation:

> "Spirit" is *pneuma*, "that part of man which knows" (1 Cor 2:11). "Soul" is *psuche*, "the seat of the affections, desires, emotions, the will, hence self," (Matt 26:38; John 12:27). "Body" is *soma*, the tabernacle, the house of the spirit and soul. The Bible makes a distinction between man's spirit, soul, and body (Gen 2:7; Heb 4:12). Man's spirit gives him God-consciousness. His soul gives him self-consciousness. His body gives him world or sense-consciousness.[15]

Similarly, *The Expositor's Greek Testament* states that "*pnuema* is put first, as the element in human nature which Paul held to be most directly allied to God, while *psuche* denotes as usual the individual life."[16]

This Pauline text should be given special priority in the issue of the soul /spirit distinction. Just as he received additional revelation about Jews and Gentiles being one spiritual body (Eph 3:1-10) and that believers who were alive at the time of the "rapture" would be instantly translated to be with Christ in glorified bodies (1 Cor 15:51), so here Paul gives greater clarity to man's three parts. J. Van Oosterzee confirms the importance of Paul's epistles in this regard.

> For Christian Dogmatics in particular it is an important question whether by the light of the Holy Scripture we must regard that personality [of man] as dichotomous or trichotomous; in other words, whether we must distinguish

man's soul from his spirit, or must consider them identical. *If we accept the teaching of St. Paul, there seems no doubt but that the question must be answered in the former sense* [trichotomy].[17]

Those who interpret 1 Thessalonians 5:23 in a straightforward manner often exhibit a devotional quality to their exposition, rather than seeing the distinguishable parts of man as a moot point. Here is an example of such exposition in this longer quote from *The Great Texts of the Bible*:

(1) The *spirit* stands first in this enumeration because the work within its unseen recesses determines the surrender of the rest of a man's powers to God's uses. This is the point at which we touch the Eternal. Just as fire came first to the altar [of the temple] and from that central point spread in mystic and broadening illumination to the outer courts, with their lamps, vessels, and sacred treasures, so, in the later dispensation, the process by which God claims men for His will and hallows their powers, begins with *the spirit*. Here is the golden altar, and God descends into soul and body by first stirring into movement those higher affinities which link our natures immediately with His own. The strict and unhalting preparation of the outward life is imperative, but the mystery through which we become God's dawns at the inmost centre of our being. We can never level ourselves up to this state by bodily acts and exercises, however intense the emotion which pervades them. Here lie the sources of character, and in sweetening these God makes the life a fragrant sacrifice. *The spirit* was designed for sovereignty over *soul and body*, and when God's fiat restores its withered powers and puts within its grasp the scepter of royalty [at regeneration], all other parts of man's nature fall into due subordination [by progressive sanctification] and attain that faultless co-adaptation of movement in which perfection consists.

(2) The sanctification of *the soul*, which is the earthen vessel containing the lower passions and appetites, follows that of the spirit. When God possesses us for His own uses, all natural instincts fulfil a Divine purpose, and fulfil it in

Man As Spirit, Soul, and Body

harmony with providential plans. The forces of the nervous life may lend virility to a man's service.

(3) It is not in its own strength and beauty that the glory of the *body* consists, but in its connection with the other parts of man. It is the servant of man's higher nature. It is the medium of communication between it and the outer world, conveying to the mind, through the senses, impressions of the outer world; and on the other hand, conveying the purpose of the higher powers of man, by means of its activity, into action in the outer world. It is in this service that the glory of *the body* consists. But the servant may become the master; this lowest part of human nature may become the ruling part. In that case *the soul*, with its strong and noble powers, becomes a shorn Samson in the lap of Delilah, and *the spirit*—that pure dove with wings of silver and feathers of yellow gold—has to lie among the pots, and bathe its breast in the mud of sensuality. Even *the body* itself, deposed from its true position and its true function, becomes degraded, and approaches towards brutality.[18]

In such devotional writing biblical psychology is integral to explaining sanctification.

Another text relevant to man's makeup as it relates to sanctification is Hebrews 4:12:

For the word of God is living and powerful, and sharper than any two-edged sword, piercing even to the division of *soul* and *spirit*, and of joints and marrow, and is a discerner of the thoughts and intents of the heart.

Here the role of the Scriptures is illustrated, which also describes the distinction between man's soul and spirit. Some trichotomists have interpreted the verse as proving that the soul and spirit can be separated from each other. (Charles Hodge's criticism of trichotomy is aimed at this more crude expression of it.)[19] Although that reading is possible, it is not required by the Greek, nor is it essential to prove trichotomy. The text probably describes the dividing of the soul and spirit together. Thiessen quoted Alford's comments on this text:

The *logos* pierces to the dividing, not of the *psuche* from the *pneuma*, but the *psuche* itself and the *pneuma* itself; the former being the lower portion of man's immaterial part, which he has in common from the brutes...the latter the higher portion, receptive to the Spirit of God...*both which are pierced and divided by the sword of the spirit, the Word of God.*[20]

The allusion seems to be that of the priest cutting open an animal for sacrifice; the knife would penetrate through the joint to the inner bone marrow. The parallel structure of soul and spirit is consistent with this concept. The joint is external to the marrow as the soul is conceptually external to the spirit in man.

Other commentators confirm the validity of the distinction of soul and spirit in this text. Thomas Hewitt states,

[The Word of God] penetrates into the deepest and most hidden parts of a man's life and dissects his lower animal life with its desires, interests, and affections, from his higher spiritual life with its aspirations for spiritual communion with God, just as a two-edged sword cuts through the joints and marrow of a physical body. [21]

While Lenski rejects a trichotomy that would allow a separate existence of the two parts of man's immaterial nature, yet he recognized a real distinction between soul and spirit.

Where, as here, [Heb 4:12] spirit and soul are distinguished, the spirit designates our immaterial part as it is related to God, as being capable of receiving the operations of the Spirit of God...The spirit ought to rule supreme; wholly controlled by God's Spirit, man ought to be *pneumatikos*. Sin enabled the *psuche* to control so that man became *psuchikos*, his bodily appetites having sway.[22]

The soul and spirit are set apart to God at conversion (positional sanctification—Heb 10:10) and are summoned to demonstrate righteous attitudes, words, and actions as an evidence of new life in Christ (progressive sanctification—Heb 10:14). Trichotomy serves to clarify this doctrine of sanctification. The precise concepts relating to the spirit and soul determine one's

Man As Spirit, Soul, and Body

understanding of the inner struggle for righteousness and God's provision for experiential holiness. In his treatment of sanctification, Heard criticized the ambiguity inherent in a non-trichotomous model of man:

> The application of the atonement as a sanctifying power is on this wise. There is in the regenerate *pneuma* a striving after holiness, as well as thirst after God. The spirit, when quickened, is that seed of God which is said by one apostle to be incorruptible (1 Pet 1:23), and by another that it cannot sin (1 John 3:9)...When the Holy Spirit of God quickens this spirit in man, and draws its desires upwards to Him, then the conflict [of flesh against spirit]...begins. Evangelical preachers who describe man as made up of two parts only, body and soul, and who say, correctly enough, that the soul, as well as the body, is desperately wicked, are therefore in a dilemma—how can a good thing come out of evil? Can a leopard change its spots, or an Ethiopian his skin? The *psuche*...is poisoned and impure; can it send forth out of the same place sweet water and bitter?[23]

In contrast to this ambiguity is the advantage of acknowledging the spirit/soul distinction. Heard continued,

> How a heart that is desperately wicked can obey godly motions is as unexplained as how a deaf man can hear or a lame man walk. Let but the distinction between *psuche* and *pneuma* be seen, and all is clear and consistent. The *psuche* is like the flesh, prone to evil, and remains so, yea, even in the regenerate. But the *pneuma* or godlike in man is not prone to evil...Its tendency is naturally upward to God, as the tendency of the body and soul is outward and earthward. Regeneration then, is the quickening of this *pneuma*, and sanctification is the carrying on of what conversion began.[24]

Sanctification was a major concern for the apostle Paul when he was inspired to write 1 Corinthians. Living in a corrupt society, the church there had fallen into many ethical problems and some heretical teachings. In the second and third chapters, the apostle identifies three categories of people: spiritual, carnal, and soulical (or soulish). The spiritual man is not only regenerated but lives in harmony with the indwelling Holy Spirit. 1 Corinthians 2:15-3:1 reads,

> But he who is *spiritual* judges all things, yet he himself is rightly judged by no one. For "who has known the mind of the LORD that he may instruct Him?" But we have the mind of Christ. And I, brethren, could not speak to you as to *spiritual* people but as to carnal, as to babes in Christ.

The spiritual man's thoughts are under the domain of God's revelation. Paul illustrated the necessity of divine revelation with a comparison to man's makeup. The role of the human spirit is specified:

> For what man knows the things of a man except the *spirit of the man* which is in him? Even so no one knows the things of God except the Spirit of God. Now we have received, not the spirit of the world, but the Spirit who is from God, that we might know the things that have been freely given to us by God (1 Cor 2:11-12).

The context goes on to rebuke the Corinthians for their neglect of spiritual growth, identifying a second class of people:

> I fed you with milk and not with solid food; for until now you were not able to receive it, and even now you are still not able; for you are still *carnal.* For where there are envy, strife, and divisions among you, are you not *carnal* and behaving like mere men? (1 Cor 3:2,3).

The word "carnal" is *sarchikoi,* literally "fleshly." The concept of flesh, when used ethically, denotes the fallen, depraved part of man which is conditioned to function independently of God. "Flesh" is closely associated with the "body of sin" (Rom 6:6) and prompts thoughts, attitudes, behaviors, and words that are in opposition to God's Holy Spirit (Gal 5:17). As the believer walks in the control and power of the Spirit of God (Gal 5:16), he will not fulfill the lusts of the flesh (Gal 5:19-21). The Spirit-filled life is essential for progress toward spiritual maturity (Heb 5:12).

The third category of people in 1 Corinthians is that of the *natural* (soulical) person:

Man As Spirit, Soul, and Body

These things we also speak, not in words which man's wisdom teaches but which the Holy Spirit teaches, comparing spiritual things with spiritual. But the natural [soulical] man does not receive the things of the Spirit of God, for they are foolishness to him; nor can he know them, because they are spiritually discerned (1 Cor 2:13,14).

The English language does not convey the precision of the Greek here. "Natural" is the rendering of *psuchikon* [soulical]. The lack of a recognized English adjective of "soulical" to correspond to "spiritual" (*pneumatikon*), and "physical" (*somatikon*), has contributed to the bias against trichotomy among English writers. Latin (and related languages) retains the original clarity with adjectives corresponding to spirit (*spiritus*) and soul (*anima*).

Richard Trench recognized the implications of the adjectives of "soulical" and "carnal" on man's makeup:

The *psuchikos* [carnal person] of Scripture is one for whom the *psuche* [soul] is the highest motive power of life and action; in whom the *pneuma* [spirit], as the organ of the divine *Pneuma*, is suppressed, dormant,...whom the operations of this divine Spirit have never lifted into the regions of spiritual things (Rom 7:14; 8:1; Jude 19).[25]

The primary reference to the natural or soulical man is to one who is unregenerate, yet the regenerate person's flesh is still prone to soulish or carnal ways of living.

James used the adjective "soulical" in his discussion about the two types of wisdom by which man can operate:

Who is wise and understanding among you? Let him show by good conduct that his works are done in the meekness of wisdom. But if you have bitter envy and self-seeking in your hearts, do not boast and lie against the truth. This wisdom does not descend from above, but is earthly, *sensual* [soulical], demonic (Jas 3:13-15).

Here "sensual" is a translation of *psuchika*. Thus, fleshly wisdom is related to the soul of man instead the divine wisdom the Spirit of God accessed through his spirit (Jas 3:17,18). Therefore, the spirit of man is the organ for the more noble functions in the regenerate person. As Heard noted,

> [Many preachers who are dichotomists], to use an illustration from physiology, seem to understand the function of spiritual-mindedness, but not to have discovered the organ which discharges that function...Function and organ are co-relative terms in physiology; they must also be in psychology.[26]

Thus, the soulish person is governed by the *psuche*: "The sensuous nature is subject to fallen man's appetite and passion (as though made up of nothing but *psuche*)."[27]

Another example of the significance of trichotomy in sanctification is the definition of "old man" as the object of co-crucifixion with Christ. Romans chapters 6-8 contain a systematic, detailed treatment of the doctrine of sanctification. Foundational to this understanding is what the believer is to "know" concerning his union with Christ: "knowing this, that our old man was crucified with Him, that the body of sin might be done away with, that we should no longer be slaves of sin" (Rom 6:6). Whereas many interpret this as positional truth only, the meaning of the believer's crucifixion with Christ will directly affect one's understanding of the basis and conditions of sanctification. Trichotomy allows for an organ in man (the spirit) that is actually changed at conversion. *Gems and Jargon* clarifies,

> At the new birth (regeneration), the unregenerate spirit or old man is crucified and replaced by the regenerate spirit or new man (new nature)...This is the logical deduction of Romans 6:3-7 where we learn that the old man was crucified resulting in death. The same passage supports a new life or new man as a result of resurrection with Christ.[28]

One's interpretation of this co-crucifixion is foundational to "reckoning" on it in daily life (Rom 6:11). Reformed writers like Martin Lloyd-Jones and John Murray have also argued convincingly for a precise definition of "old man" that is distinct from "sin," "flesh," "old ego," or "sin nature." Lloyd-Jones wrote,

> I trust that this distinction between the "old man" and the "body of sin" is clear. It is most important. That is why

I have contended so much against the idea that the "old man" means the "old nature," and that the "old man" and the "body of sin" are one and the same thing. If you believe that, you will still be in bondage...You do not die to that old man; the old man is not going through the process of dying; he has died, and he has been buried, he has gone once and forever, he is finished. You are a new man in Christ.[29]

John Murray likewise affirmed,

It is a mistake to think of the believer as both an old man and a new man or as having in him both the old man and the new man, the latter in view of regeneration and the former because of remaining corruption. That this is not Paul's conception is made apparent here by the fact that the "old man" is represented as having been crucified with Christ and the tense indicates a once-for-all definitive act [aorist tense].[30]

Murray maintains this distinction yet defines the old man as "the old self or ego, the unregenerate man in his entirety in contrast to the new man as the regenerate in his entirety."[31] Whereas the clarifications of Murray and Loyd-Jones regarding the "old man's" death are beneficial, their dichotomist orientation seems to shift the ambiguity from the "old man" to how this "new man" struggles with indwelling sin (1 Pet 2:11; Rom 7:14-24). Nevertheless, their precision on the "old man" as distinct from the "flesh" is welcome. This insight was influential in David Needham's research on the implications of the believer's identity in Christ. In appendix B of *Birthright*, Needham gives a thorough treatment of the terms "old man" and "flesh" concluding that they are not synonymous. The "old man" was crucified with Christ; the "flesh" continues as a source of antagonism to the things of God. [32]

Another example of how the trichotomous model of man clarifies the doctrine of progressive sanctification is the interpretation of 1 John 3:9, which states: "Whoever has been born of God does not sin, for His seed remains in him; and he cannot sin, because he has been born of God." This is a puzzling text for commentators because earlier John stated: "If we say that we have no sin, we deceive ourselves, and the truth is not in us" (1 John 1:8). Without going into detail about the antinomian lifestyle of the false teachers then (1 John 2:26; 3:7), John warned that the true believer would demonstrate his faith through love and good works (1 John 5:1,2). Yet, the text of 1 John 3:9 indicates a more radical trait of the believer: "...he cannot sin because he has been born of God. In his sequel to *Birthright* Needham reasons,

> But what did John mean by "cannot sin"? When John used the word "cannot," I believe he was trying to communicate a critical point. Sinning...is so utterly irrational [for the regenerate]—so stupid—no one in their right mind would even consider sinning a reasonable behavior...Sinning would still be reasonable if one-half of your essential nature were sinful. But nowhere in John's epistle did he suggest that a Christian was a "two-dispositioned" person.[33]

For the trichotomist, the "seed" of God's Spirit would have its locus in the regenerate human spirit; sin would henceforth not originate from the believer's spirit, but from the flesh, the world and the devil. Because of this, Paul could declare "For I delight in the law of God according to the inward man [the new spirit]" (Rom 7:22).

Although Needham quotes sources both for and against trichotomy, he eventually affirms some distinctions within man's immaterial side:

> All of us are used to functioning with "levels of self."...It is not therefore so strange to affirm that for the believer there is a deeper level of self than either of these [conscious mind and unconscious mind]—spirit...No, I am not two people, but there are most certainly levels to my personhood. There is a deep level of self (inner man) and my more shallow level.[34]

The trichotomist would identify this "deep level" as spirit and the more "shallow level" as soul. David Kerr confirms that this distinctive use of spirit is represented throughout Scripture:

> In both Testaments it is man's spirit which is the spring of his inmost thoughts and intents, and the child of God must be renewed in spirit if he is to serve God acceptably (Ps 51:10 ff.; Gal 5:22; 1 John 4:13).[35]

Man As Spirit, Soul, and Body

The role of the body in sanctification requires it to be used as "an instrument of righteousness" (Rom 6:13). Paul exemplified this through disciplining his body, making it the slave of his inner person (1 Cor 9:27). The authority of sin was broken through the believer's identification with Christ in His death, burial, resurrection, and ascension. The result of this new spiritual relationship is that the body of sin should be rendered inoperative as a tool for sin (Rom 6:6). These cautions about the physical body are not due to its material nature (as in Greek dualism), but because of the effects of the Fall.

Physical Death

It has been noted in the evaluation of monism that the soul and spirit separate from the body at physical death; this proves that man has more than one part. Paul stated his hope in Philippians 1:21-23:

> For to me, to live is Christ, and to die is gain. But if I live on in the flesh, this will mean fruit from my labor; yet what I shall choose I cannot tell. For I am pressed between the two, having a desire to depart and be with Christ, which is far better.

Paul anticipated being in God's presence immediately following death:

> So we are always confident, knowing that while we are at home in the body we are absent from the Lord. For we walk by faith, not by sight. We are confident, yes, well pleased rather to be absent from the body and to be present with the Lord" (2 Cor 5:6-8).

Heard reasoned that dichotomy seems to imply the false teaching of soul sleep. In contrast, he presented a rationale for conscious existence in the intermediate state:

> We have described the three parts of man's nature, as three kinds or degrees of consciousness. There is sense-consciousness, or the animal body; self-consciousness, or the rational soul; God-consciousness, or the Spirit [spirit]. We have also seen that it is conceivable, that any two of these

forms of consciousness could exist without the presence and co-operation of the remaining third; the first and second without the third; or the second and third without the first. As two chords in music will make harmony, but not less than two, so either the animal or the rational, or the rational and the spiritual, will combine to sustain what we call life or consciousness in man.[36]

Thus, after the Fall man existed with his spirit separated from the life of God; after death he exists as soul and spirit separated from the body.

Various references point to man's conscious existence after death. The parable of the rich man and Lazarus vividly describes this (Luke 16:19-31). Even with allowance for symbolic elements in the parable, the story affirms man's conscious existence after death. Hebrews includes a vision of the redeemed in heaven as "the spirits of just men made perfect" (Heb 12:23). Without the "body of sin" and the environment of a world system hostile to God, believers are blessed with perfected sanctification. Although the genre is apocalyptic, Revelation 6:9,10 teaches the conscious existence of believers after death:

> When He opened the fifth seal, I saw under the altar the souls of those who had been slain for the word of God and for the testimony which they held. And they cried with a loud voice, saying, "How long, O Lord, holy and true, until You judge and avenge our blood on those who dwell on the earth?"

Dichotomists draw attention to the use of "souls" in this passage, whereas "spirits" are referred to in Hebrews 12:23. This, however, does not contradict trichotomy; both the soul and spirit form man's immaterial nature. There is no evidence that they are ever separated. On the other hand, the connotation of these terms is consistent with the meanings affirmed by trichotomists. In Hebrews, the writer mentions "spirit" because of the association with God and the assembly of the Firstborn; in Revelation the context is that of martyrdom, which would more closely relate to the body and therefore "soul" is used.

Man As Spirit, Soul, and Body

Bodily Resurrection

Whereas the resurrection is chronologically future, it belongs in the context of redemption *history* because it has been revealed in the past, and because it is an accomplished fact in the mind of God (Rom 8:30). The resurrection of the just and the unjust is promised throughout Scripture (Dan 12:2; John 5:28,29; 1 Thes 4:13-18; Phil 3:20,21). The resurrection of the body indicates that man is a unified being; the intermediate state is abnormal.

The predictions about the believer's resurrection in 1 Corinthians 15:35-55 include important references that relate to the makeup of man:

> The body is sown in corruption, it is raised in incorruption. It is sown in dishonor, it is raised in glory. It is sown in weakness, it is raised in power. It is sown a *natural* body, it is raised a *spiritual* body. There is a *natural* body, and there is a *spiritual* body (1 Cor 15:42-44).

The mortal body is called "natural" translating *soma psuchikon* (soulical body); the resurrection body is called "spiritual" translating *soma pneumatikon* (spiritual body). Why is the mortal body described as "soulical"? Pember observed, "...while the soul is the meeting-point of the elements of our being in this present life, the spirit will be the ruling power in our resurrection state."[37]

Adam and Christ are also contrasted in this passage:

> And so it is written, "The first man Adam became a living being." The last Adam became a life-giving spirit. However, the *spiritual* is not first, but the *natural,* and afterward the *spiritual.* The first man was of the earth, made of dust; the second Man is the Lord from heaven. As was the man of dust, so also are those who are made of dust; and as is the heavenly Man, so also are those who are heavenly (1 Cor 15:45-48).

Adam was identified by "soul" (living being); Christ was identifying as a "life-giving spirit." As made spiritually alive by Christ (Who is the last Adam), the believer becomes conformed to the image of Christ even to glorification. According to verse 46, the former state was "natural" (*to psuchikon*). This confirms the other passages that identify the natural condition of man on earth as under the sway of the soul, rather than the spirit (1 Cor 2:14; Jas 3:15; Jude 19). *The resurrected body is spiritual,* radically changed by Christ—the "life-giving spirit."

The soulical nature of man supplies the naturally dominant influence of this present body of humiliation; however, the spirit will be the identified center of the resurrection body.[38] Heard stated,

> The resurrection body is thus spiritual, not carnal, and if spiritual, then *the spirit* and not the animal [soulical] nature, which we lay in the grave, is to be regarded as the nucleus around which it will gather.[39]

Austin-Sparks noted that the resurrection unto life,

> is that of a spiritual body, the consummation or full fruit of a spiritual life. In light of this, how important it is to know the difference between soul and spirit; between religion as a thing of the soul, and true spirituality as from Christ within, Who alone is the "hope of glory."[40]

The resurrection of the body is both a confirmation of the primary unity of human beings and an evidence of their two separable elements. The Greek adjectives denoting "soulical" and "spiritual" give further evidence of the distinction of the two aspects of the immaterial element as well as the contrasting characteristics of the fallen and glorified body.

Summary

Thus, the distinctions between man's spirit, soul, and body are relevant to the exposition of many Scripture passages related to the full scope of redemption. The previous chapter of biblical word studies supports this exegesis of relevant Scriptures. We have sketched here how the tripartite model of man illumines the meaning of his creation, Fall, regeneration, sanctification, and eventual glorification. Having briefly traced the implications of trichotomy through redemptive history, the next chapter will note its place in church history.

[1] J. B. Heard, *The Tripartite Nature of Man*, 40.

[2] Thomas D. Bernard, *The Progress of Doctrine in the New Testament* (Grand Rapids: Eerdmans, 1949), 39.

[3] Ed Bulkley, *Why Christians Can't Trust Psychology* (Eugene, OR: Harvest House, 1993), 339.

[4] Delitzsch, *A System of Biblical Psychology*, 95.

[5] John McClintock and John Strong, *Cyclopedia of Biblical, Theological, and Ecclesiastical Literature*, s.v. "Spirit" (Grand Rapids: Baker Book House, 1981 reprint from 1887), 9:944.

[6] Lehman Strauss, *Man a Trinity* in *Death and Afterward* (Biblical Studies Press, 1997), 4. Ray C. Stedman gives a similar trichotomous interpretation of Genesis 2:7 in *Understanding Man* (Portland, OR: Multnomah Press, 1975), 26.

[7] Wayne Grudem, *Systematic Theology* (Grand Rapids: Zondervan, 1994), 447.

[8] Herbert Lockyer, *All the Doctrines of the Bible* (Grand Rapids: Zondervan, 1964), 145.

[9] J. D. Douglas, ed., *The New International Dictionary of the Christian Church* [NIDCC], Revised ed., (Grand Rapids: Zondervan, 1978), s.v. "Luther," by Carl S. Meyer, 610.

[10] Austin-Sparks, *What is Man?*, 22,24. Cf. Ian Thomas, *The Indwelling Life of Chirst* (Colorado Springs: Multnomah Books, 2006) 36.

[11] Berkhof, *Systematic Theology*, 469.

[12] Pember, *Earth's Earliest Ages*, 77. H. D. Edmond noted that the human spirit is present in unregenerate man, but is dead toward God: "Through his spirit, man reaches up to the spiritual world, Godward. The fallen man has an awareness of the reality of God and the spiritual, but in his unregenerate condition he has no direct contact with God. Thus the unregenerate man can only understand a religion of the senses. With the new birth he is brought into direct relation with God through the renewed spirit, enabling him to worship God in spirit and truth." —*The Thessalonian Epistles* (Chicago: Moody Press, 1971) 253.

[13] Robert Jamieson, A. R. Fausset, and David Brown, *Commentary on the Whole Bible*, Revised ed. (Grand Rapids: Zondervan, 1961), 1339; cf. Gordon Fee, *God's Empowering Presence, The Holy Spirit in the Letters of Paul*, 66.

[14] Heard, *The Tripartite Nature of Man*, 76.

[15] John Linberry, *Vital Word Studies in 1 Thessalonians* (Grand Rapids: Zondervan, 1960), 127. See similar expositions and definitions of the trichotomy of spirit, soul, and body: William Kelly, *The Epistle of Paul the Apostle to the 1 and 2 Thessalonians*, 73,74; Fredrick A. Tatford, *Paul's Letter to the Thessalonians* (Neptune, NJ: Loizeaux Bros, 1990), 74,75; John Lillie, *Lectures on the Epistles of Paul to the Thessalonians* (NY: Robert Carter & Bros, 1860), 397,398; Paul Ellingsworth and Eugene Nida, *Paul's Letters to the Thessalonians: U.B.S. Handbook* (NY: United Bible Societies, 1976), 126; James Hastings, ed. *The Great Texts of the Bible* (Grand Rapids: Eerdmans), 18:52,53; Charles John Ellicott, ed. *Bible Commentary*; A. J. Mason, *1 Thessalonians* (NY: Cassell & Co.) 8:146., H.A. Ironside, *Addresses on the 1 & 2 Epistles of the Thessalonians* (Neptune, NJ: Loizeaux Bros), 73; Donald Grey Barnhouse, *Thessalonians*, (Zondervan, 1977), 104. Ellicott remarked that the interpretation that views spirit, soul, and body here as merely a rhetorical piling up of words for emphasis, plainly sets aside "all sound rules of scriptural exegesis."—H. D. Edmond, *The Thessalonian Epistles*, (Chicago: Moody Press, 1971), 252.

[16] W. Robertson Nicoll, *The Expositor's Greek Testament* (Eerdmans, 1951), 4:43.

[17] J. J. Van Oosterzee, *Church Dogmatics*, Trans. J. Watson and M. Evan (NY: Scribner, Armstrong, & Co., 1874), 2:365,66 [Emphasis added].

[18] James Hastings, ed. *The Great Texts of the Bible* (Grand Rapids: Eerdmans), 18:53-54 [Emphasis added].

[19] Charles Hodge, *Systematic Theology* (Grand Rapids: Eerdmans, 1979), 2:50.

[20] Thiessen, *Introductory Lectures in Systematic Theology*, 227 [Emphasis added].

[21] Thomas Hewitt, *The Epistle to the Hebrews*, Tyndale New Testament Commentaries, ed., R. V. G. Tasker (London: Intervarsity Press, 1974), 15:90.

[22] R. C. H. Lenski, *The Interpretation of St. Paul's Epistles to the Thessalonians* (Minneapolis, MN: Augsburg, 1964), 367.

[23] Heard, *The Tripartite Nature of Man*, 217.

[24] Ibid., 218.

[25] Richard C. Trench, *Synonyms of the New Testament* (Grand Rapids: Eerdmans, 1963), 269.

[26] Heard, *The Tripartite Nature of Man*, 18,19.

[27] Thayer, *Psuchikos*, Greek-English Lexicon, 678.

[28] Charles R. Solomon and H. David Clark, *Gems and Jargon* (Lakewood CO: Cross-Life Expressions 1980), 9.

[29] D. Martin Lloyd-Jones, *Romans: The New Man* (Grand Rapids: Zondervan, 1972), 6:78.

[30] John Murray, *The Epistle to the Romans* (Grand Rapids: Eerdmans, 1968), 1:220.

[31] Ibid., 219.

[32] David C. Needham, *Birthright* (Portland, OR: Multnomah Press, 1979), 239-63.

[33] David C. Needham, *Alive for the First Time* (Portland, OR: Multnomah, 1995), 91.

[34] Ibid., 106-07.

[35] David H. Kerr, *Spirit*, in *Baker's Dictionary of Theology* (Grand Rapids: Baker Book House, 1960), 493.

[36] Heard, *The Tripartite Nature of Man*, 268.

[37] Pember, *Earth's Earliest Ages*, 75. By way of contrast, Arnold Fruchtenbaum's paper on dichotomy *The Composition of Man* (Ariel Ministries, 1985), 6, disregards the soul/spirit distinction deduced from the use of these adjectives by asserting that in 1 Corinthians 15 the same body is referred to in both cases. However, even though there is a continuity between the mortal and immortal body, the intrinsic differences in their characteristics more than support their

contrasting natures as soulical (mortal body) and spiritual (resurrected body).

38 Heard, *The Tripartite Nature of Man*, 84.

39 Ibid., 342-43 [Emphasis added].

40 Austin-Sparks, *What is Man?*, 98.

Chapter 5
Trichotomy in Church History

The Record of the Early Church

Various fathers of the early church believed in a spirit, soul, and body distinction in man. Dichotomists tend to discredit this testimony by attributing it to the influence of Greek philosophy. Marais made this connection in an article on biblical psychology: "Under the influence of Platonic philosophy, trichotomy found favor in the early church."[1] Yet, the trichotomy of Plato differed significantly from biblical trichotomy. As Heard pointed out,

> Plato, the intellectualist, assigned to reason or nous the sovereign place [in man's makeup]; but...in Scripture psychology the intellect holds the second place not the first. To harmonize Plato and St. Paul together is impossible. The appetitive nature of Plato corresponds, we admit, to the body or animal nature of St. Paul (1 Thes 5:23). But the *psuche* of St. Paul is distributed by Plato between the emotional and intellectual natures seated in the heart and head respectively, while the *pneuma* of St. Paul is unknown to Plato.[2]

Thus, Plato's model of trichotomy was body, soul, and *mind* (not spirit).

Platonic trichotomy is further removed from a biblical one due to Plato's view of the three parts of soul. As Richard Norris observed,

> For Plato...the human soul is in fact tripartite. Its two lower, and mortal parts are the seats of desire and of assertive

action; its superior part, the rational (*to logistikon*), shares with the world-soul the attributes of incorruptibility.[3]

To discredit trichotomy by a similarity with Platonism confuses similarity with source. One could likewise attribute the source of the dichotomist view with Greek dualism of matter and spirit; some writers have argued for such a connection.[4]

The trichotomous view was considered an orthodox interpretation in the first three centuries of the church. Theologian Luis Berkhof summarized this record:

> The trichotomic conception of man found considerable favor with the Greek or Alexandrian Church Fathers in the early Christian centuries. It is found, though not always in the same form, in Clement of Alexandria, Origen, and Gregory of Nyssa. But after Apollinaris employed it in a manner impinging on the perfect humanity of Jesus, it was gradually discredited. Some of the Greek Fathers still adhered to it, though Athanasius and Theodoret explicitly repudiated it. In the Latin Church the leading theologians distinctly favored the twofold division of human nature. It was the psychology of Augustine that gave prominence to this view.[5]

Heard cited additional sources for trichotomy in the early church:

> Irenaeus, Justin Martyr, Clement of Alexandria, Origen, Didymus of Alexandria, Gregory of Nyssa, and Basil of Caesarea all note the distinction between soul and spirit, and designate the spirit as that which bears the truest image of God.[6]

An example from the Eastern Church would be John of Damascus, who spoke of the soul as being the sensuous life-principle that takes up the spirit (which is the "efflux" of God).[7]

Herbert Lockyer documented early expressions of trichotomy. He quoted Justin Martyr's comparison: "As the body is the house of the soul, so the soul is the house of the spirit." Lockyer also mentioned another analogy used in the past:

Man As Spirit, Soul, and Body

The ancients had a fitting way of illustrating the threefold possession of man. They likened the body to the material framework of a chariot—the soul, with all its powers, to the horses driving the chariot along—the spirit, to the charioteer, whose firm hands held the reins and whose keen eyes determined the course.[8]

Lockyer commented on the implications of this view of man:

If the spirit part of man is inoperative, or under the control of evil spirits...then there is chaos, tragedy, and death, for God meant the body to be the servant of the soul, and the soul the servant of the spirit.[9]

A factor that hindered the Church's acceptance of trichotomy was its reaction to dualism. Plato's view of the soul as preexistent and superior to the material body denied the doctrine of creation *ex nihilo*. In the third century Manichaeism advocated a radical dualism in cosmology and in man. Rather than the wrestling with subtleties of the soul/spirit distinction, the fathers addressed the issue of man's basic unity, in contrast to these dualistic philosophies. As Rodney Hunter summarized it,

They held to the doctrine of the Resurrection as descriptive of the destiny intended by God for humanity: Both body and soul were destined for immortality since the person functions as a living whole.[10]

Even after the Church followed Augustine in favoring dichotomy, the Eastern Church continued to favor trichotomy.

The Heresy of Apollinaris

Since the view of Apollinaris marks the decline in the acceptance of trichotomy in the Western Church, his teaching deserves closer inspection. This bishop of Laodicea in Syria affirmed the orthodoxy of Christ's deity and humanity as expressed in Nicene Creed. The difficulty, however, was the way he tried to explain how Christ's humanity was constituted through His incarnation. W. Walker summarized Apollinaris' view:

Jesus had the body and animal soul of man, but that the reasoning spirit in Him was the *logos*. By this he [Apollinaris] meant that the highest directing principle of His existence could not be a human mind, but must be divine. For Apollinaris the human mind is corrupt and in the service of the flesh. In consequence it must have been replaced in Jesus by the *logos*.[11]

This view was interpreted as denying the full humanity of Christ, and was condemned at the Second Ecumenical Council in Constantinople in A.D. 381. The view of Apollinaris influenced the Eastern Church and even in the west it was eventually conceded that, although Christ's mind was human, His center was not that of man but the *Logos* Himself.[12] Rather than deal with the subtleties of the soul/spirit distinction, Augustine opted for dichotomy. Since he has been one of Christianity's most influential thinkers, Augustine's view became dominant in the west.

The Trichotomy of Luther

Most of the scholars of the Reformation continued to hold to the dichotomous view of man. Berkhof noted the trend of dichotomy from the days of Augustine (in the fourth century) through the Protestant Reformation (in the 16th century).

During the Middle Ages it [dichotomy] became a matter of common belief. The Reformation brought no change in this respect, though a few lesser lights defended the trichotomistic theory.[13]

Instead of looking at these "lesser lights," an examination of Martin Luther's view illustrates the reluctance of contemporary theologians to acknowledge trichotomy as a legitimate view during the Reformation.

In his commentary on the Gospel of Luke, Luther gave a detailed explanation of the parts of man when he discussed Mary's Magnificat: "My soul magnifies the Lord, and my spirit has rejoiced in God my Savior" (Luke 1:46). Luther wrote,

Let us take up the words in their order. The first is "my soul." Scripture divides man into three parts, as St. Paul says in 1 Thessalonians 5:23...The nature of man consists of the three parts—spirit, soul, and body...The first part, the spirit, is the highest, deepest, and noblest part of man. By it he is enabled to lay hold on things incomprehensible, invisible, and eternal. It is, in brief, the dwelling place of faith and the Word of God.[14]

This quotation shows that the Reformer recognized an ontological distinction of the spirit from the soul. Luther's reference to 1 Thessalonians 5:23 gives further support to his basic definition of trichotomy.

One might wonder why Luther's trichotomous teaching has been virtually ignored. One reason may be that his references to the soul as the immaterial element (in contrast to the body) have been taken as evidence of dichotomy in his writings. In the same context, his definition of soul as immaterial exemplifies this:

The second part, the soul, is this same spirit, so far as its [immaterial] nature is concerned, but viewed as performing a different function, namely, giving life to the body and working through the body.[15]

In his *Systematic Theology*, Strong gave a footnote to Luther's trichotomous statements, noting that Franz Delitzsch also quoted this passage in his *System of Biblical Psychology*. Yet, Strong hastened to refer to Thomasius' argument for Luther as dichotomous. Thomasius's argument, however, primarily rests on the preceding quote, which merely describes the soul as immaterial. This being the case, it is vital to rightly examine Luther's teaching on the model of man in the context of this description to the soul. When Luther said that the soul is the same "nature" (German—*natur*) he was affirming what trichotomists concede as well, i.e., that the soul and spirit are united as the immaterial side of human nature. In the same paragraph that he defined "soul", Luther continued to elucidate the distinction between soul and spirit:

It is its [the soul's] nature to comprehend not incomprehensible things but such things the reason can know and understand. Indeed, reason is the light of this dwelling; and unless the spirit, which is lighted with the brighter light of faith, controls this light of reason it cannot but be in error. For it is too feeble to deal with things divine. To these two parts of man [spirit and soul] the Scriptures ascribe many things, such as wisdom and knowledge—wisdom to the spirit, knowledge to the soul.[16]

This shows that Luther believed the distinction between soul and spirit to be more than merely one of connotation or function. The term "part" is used eight times in this context in denoting the parts of man (spirit, soul, and body). The German term Luther used was teil, meaning "part," "division," or "portion."[17] He also used the synonym *stuck*, meaning "piece," "part," or "portion."[18] However uncomfortable to the ears of the proponents of monism or monistic dualism, Luther did not hesitate to speak in terms of the three parts of a person.

After noting the distinction of the body, Luther gave a profound analogy relating to the tabernacle. What seems at first glance to be an unusual comparison becomes increasingly meaningful. Luther continued,

Let us take an illustration from the Scriptures. In the tabernacle fashioned by Moses there were three separate compartments. The first was called the holy of holies: here was God's dwelling place, and in it there was no light. The second was called the holy place; here stood a candlestick with seven arms and seven lamps. The third was called the outer court; this lay under the open sky and in the full light of the sun. In this tabernacle we have a figure of the Christian man. His spirit is the holy of holies, where God dwells in the darkness of faith, where no light is; for he believes that which he neither sees nor feels nor comprehends. His soul is the holy place, with its seven lamps, that is, all manner of reason, discrimination, knowledge, and understanding of visible and bodily things. His body is the forecourt, open to all, so that men may see his works and manner of life.[19]

Luther continued by drawing attention to the priority of man's spirit in sanctification. Expounding again on 1 Thessalonians 5:23, he even took note of the sequence Paul mentioned:

Man As Spirit, Soul, and Body

When the *spirit* that possesses the whole inheritance is pre-served, both *soul* and *body* are able to remain without er-ror and evil works. On the other hand, when the *spirit* is without faith, the *soul* together with the whole life cannot but fall into wickedness and error...As a consequence of this error and false opinion of the soul, all the works of the body also become evil and damnable, even though a man killed himself with fasting and performed the works of all the saints...it is necessary that God preserve, first *our spirit*, then *our soul and body*, not only from overt sins but more from false and apparent good works.[20]

Thus, Luther clearly connected trichotomy of man with the bib-lical strategy for progressive sanctification.

The Resurgence of Trichotomy

There were also notable cases of trichotomist writing in the 17th and 18th centuries. An example of this view of man in the 17th century was the influential *A Method of Prayer*, by Madame Guyon. This text of mystical piety, although arousing opposition by church authorities in France, endured to inspire Christian leaders in subsequent centuries, including John Wes-ley, Jessie Penn-Lewis, and Watchman Nee.[21] In 1769, M. F. Roos published in Latin a scholarly expression of trichotomy.[22]

The 19th century featured a resurgence of trichotomy by several British and German theologians. From Britain came J. B. Heard's *The Tripartite Nature of Man*, and J. T. Beck's *Outlines of Biblical Psychology*. In Germany were Olshausen, Lotze, Gos-chel, Auberian, Delitzsch (who wrote the often-quoted *A System of Biblical Psychology*), and G. F. Oehler (who authored *Theology of the Old Testament*). Other works that affirmed this model of man included Ellicott's *Destiny of the Creature*, and Van Ooster-zee's *Christian Dogmatics*.[23] These scholars' volumes advanced trichotomy as biblical, reasonable, and relevant to Christian life and ministry.

Sir George Gabriel Stokes (1819-1903) was a professor at Cambridge University for over fifty years. Stokes proposed:

...that man consisted of body, soul and spirit, rather than the dual nature consisting of only body and soul. The dual nature of man was first put forth by Plato, not the Bible, according to Stokes, and he believed that the concept was propagated by theologians and philosophers who did not go back to the source. For Stokes, the spirit was the element that provided the life essence to the body and it survived death. The difficulty for him was explaining the difference between spirit and soul. But he also believed that the source for this knowledge was revelation and not reason.[24]

The 20th century featured additional theologians who have advocated trichotomy. Systematic theology texts supporting trichotomy include volumes by E. H. Bankcroft, H. C. Thiessen, L. S. Chafer, M. Cambron, P. B. Fitzwater, H. Lockyer, and F. H. Barackman. Other trichotomist volumes on Biblical anthropology include G. H. Pember's *Earth's Earliest Ages*, L. T. Holdcroft's *Anthropology: a Biblical View*, Jessie Penn-Lewis' *Soul and Spirit*, Oswald Chamber's *Biblical Psychology*, T. Austin-Spark's *What is Man?*, Watchman Nee's *The Spiritual Man*, and Dale Moody's *The Word of Truth*.

Bible conferences have been communicating this devotional truth through a trichotomous model of man. For example, the Keswick convention, which began in England in the late 1800's, has taught the deeper life through an explicit trichotomous view of man. Evan Hopkins' writings exemplified the movement; he supported trichotomy with several quotes from Delizsch's book.[25] Prominent evangelical ministries such as Christian Literature Crusade, Capernwray Missionary Fellowship, and the Institute in Basic Life Principles have been communicating the abundant life with the trichotomous model of man. Mor examples will be presented in Chapter 8.

Summary

The theological vindication of trichotomy in the 19th century gave fertile soil to a variety of authors and ministries that have taught from this perspective in the 20th century. Although it has gained popularity in more fundamental circles and on a popular level, the majority of evangelical systematic theologians have maintained the dichotomist viewpoint. To further address this disparity, the next chapter will present a biblical and theological case for holistic trichotomy.

[1] Marais, *Psychology*, ISBE, 4:2496.

[2] Heard, *The Tripartite Nature of Man*, 64.

[3] Richard A. Norris, *Soul*, in *Encyclopedia of Early Christianity*, 2d ed. (NY: Garland Publishers, 1997).

[4] Heard, *The Tripartite Nature of Man*, 7.

[5] Berkhof, *Systematic Theology*, 191.

[6] Heard, *The Tripartite Nature of Man*, 4. In the second century, Melito of Sardis wrote *Concerning the Soul, the Body and the Mind*. This work was later quoted by Eusebius and Jerome. (Dallas Willard, *The Spirit of the Disciplines*, 112.)

[7] Strong, *Systematic Theology*, 487.

[8] Lockyer, *All the Doctrines of the Bible*, 144-45.

[9] Ibid., 145. Psychiatrist, Rama P. Coomarawamy, observed that Dante (1265-1321), author of *The Divine Comedy*, saw man as endowed with threefold life: "vegetable, animal and rational, and hence he walks a triple path. Inasmuch as he is a vegetable, he seeks utility, in *quo cum plantis communicat*; inasmuch as he is an animal, he seeks pleasure in which he participates with brutes; inasmuch as he is rational, he seeks for honor, in which he is either alone, or is associated with the angels, *vel angelicae naturae sociatur* (*De Vulg. Eloq.* ii. 2)."

[10] Rodney J. Hunter, ed., *Dictionary of Pastoral Care and Counseling* (Nashville: Abingdon Press, 1990), s.v. "Soul," by R. A. Muller, 1202.

[11] Williston Walker, *A History of the Christian Church*, 3d ed., (NY: Charles Scribner's Sons, 1970), 132.

[12] Ibid. Centuries later, Thomas Aquinas exemplified the persistence of dichotomy in the western church. In his appendix, "Pagan Philosophy and its View of Man's Soul," Gene Edwards traces the loss of trichotomy of man in church history and the resulting intellectualizing of the faith. *The Highest Life* (Tyndale House, 1989), 167-88.

[13] Berkhof, *Systematic Theology*, 192.

[14] Martin Luther, *Luther's Works*, ed., Jaroslar Pelikan (St. Louis: Concordia, 1956), 21:303. McClintock and Strong noted that trichoto-

my was still held by evangelical Lutherans in the late 1800's—*Cyclopedia of Ecclesiastical Literature*, 10:549.

[15] Ibid.

[16] Ibid.

[17] Muret-Sanders *Encyclopedic English–German and German–English Dictionary*, 1910 ed., s.v. "Tiel," 2:952.

[18] Ibid., s.v. "Stuck," 937.

[19] Luther, *Luther's Works*, 304.

[20] Ibid., 305-06 [Emphasis added].

[21] Jeanne Guyon, *Experiencing the Depths of Jesus Christ*, edited by Gene Edwards (Goleta, CA: Christian Books, 1975), 145-50.

[22] Clark, *The Biblical Doctrine of Man*, 43.

[23] Strong, *Systematic Theology*, 484.

[24]lucasianchair.org/stokes.html, based on David Wilson, "A physicist's alternative to materialism: the religious thought of George Gabriel Stokes," Victorian Studies 28 (Autumn 1984): 71-84.

[25] Evan H. Hopkins, *The Law of Liberty in the Spiritual Life*, American ed. (Fort Washington, PA: Christian Literature Crusade, 1991), 47, 49, 58-60. Many in the Keswick tradition have taught trichotomy, including Andrew Murray (*The Spirit of Christ*) and F. B. Meyer. The latter wrote, "The soul opens upward to the Infinite and Eternal through the Spirit, with its capacity for God, and downward to the Finite and Temporal through the Body, with its capacity for material objects. The spirit stands for our heavenly aptitudes, the body for our earthly ones. By the one we are able to seek things that are above, where Christ is, seated on the right of God; through the other we are apt to become entangled with the things that pertain to earth" (Col. 3: 1-5). *The Soul's Pure Intention*, 5. Ian Thomas' *The Mystery of Godliness*, presents a grace-oriented explanation of sanctification with an explicit trichotomy and diagrams. Thomas' teaching ministry is foundational to the international Bible schools of the Capernwray Missionary Fellowship.

Chapter 6
Holistic Trichotomy

Holistic Trichotomy Proposed

Before answering some traditional criticisms of trichotomy, this model of man needs to be defined more precisely. Delitzsch and Heard differentiated true and false versions of trichotomy. Dichotomist Gordon Clark acknowledged that some writers have refuted a crude form of trichotomy, yet he was not aware of any current proponents of a less objectionable form of it. He compared trichotomy to man's consisting of three separable elements. Using an example from chemistry, he compared dichotomy to a compound like NaCl, but withheld biblical approval of this analogy (while maintaining dichotomy).[1] He then compared trichotomy to a compound of three elements—H_2SO_4. It seems this crude analogy can stigmatize trichotomy without a similar objection to dichotomy. This raises the issue of the need to define terms accurately and clarify a model of trichotomy that does not go beyond what is written in Scripture. This book advocates an expression of this doctrine which is designated "holistic trichotomy."

The first aspect of this model is an affirmation of man's basic unity. Physical death, which separates the soul from the body until the resurrection, is an abnormal state; it is outside of God's primary design for man. Hence, the Hebrew perspective of man's primary unity is valued. A human is "one" in regard to personhood, identity, responsibility, and ultimate destiny. Although Paul distinguished sin in the believer's members as distinct from the ego, he did not absolve the individual of personal responsibility for his/her actions (Rom 7:17). The detailed study on the soul and spirit in this book is not intended to emphasize a separation within man. If the contrast of three and one in this nomenclature of holistic trichotomy is disapproved by a dichotomist, it should be noticed that terms such as "conditional unity" and "psychosomatic unity" (designations of dichotomy) are no less problematic to the monist.

The more difficult task is to find terms that accurately convey the degree of distinction between spirit, soul, and body. Theologians have used a variety of expressions in defining the soul's distinction (or lack of it) from the spirit. Phrases describing the soul include "constituent part" (Hoekema), "substantive entity" (Buswell), "substance" or "part" (Strong), "essential element" (Hodge), and "constituent element" (Berkhof). These authors do not regard soul and spirit to be distinct parts according to these terms; they view the soul and spirit as having a functional rather than an ontological distinction. Trichotomists have used terms such as "parts," "elements," "substances," "natures," "portions," "aspects," and "components." Thus, it is necessary to clarify the terms used in defining a model of man. Many traditional terms are misleading; they conceptualize the spirit as a separate, different substance. The doctrine of the Trinity affirms God's unity in substance and essence, yet recognizes the distinction of His persons [*hypostases*]: Father, Son, and Holy Spirit. Similarly, the trichotomist affirms man's spirit/soul to be one snon-material element yet with differing qualities.

Some have insisted that for man to have three parts, the parts must necessarily be capable of separation and autonomous existence. However, holistic trichotomy concedes that the wording of Hebrews 4:12, "the division of soul and spirit," does not require the possibility of soul and spirit having a separate existence. Therefore, the soul cannot exist apart from the spirit in the way body and soul can. Holistic trichotomy avoids the objection of scholars who argue that man has only two elements or sides (body and soul). Likewise, the ontological distinction between soul and spirit does not require that they be distinct in substance; the soul contains the spirit and both share an immaterial nature (see page 136). Delitzsch acknowledged this in distinguishing the spirit from the soul, but not designating the spirit as a separate, autonomous entity.

Holistic trichotomy accepts the fundamental duality in the individual as body and soul; man is both material and immaterial, physical and non-physical, corporeal and non-corporeal. Norman Geisler's *Systematic Theology* seems to balance man's essential unity with the duality of his *separable* parts.

> Each individual human being is a unity of soul and body, having a spiritual dimension and a physical dimension. Each partakes of the immaterial as well as the material, the angelic as well as the animal. As such, human beings are unique: each is a psychosomatic unity, a blend of mind and matter.[2]

Yet, Geisler proceeded to include a distinction of soul and spirit in the immaterial side of man:

> Paul speaks of "spirit, soul, and body" forming an individual "wholly" (1 Thes 5:23); that is, these three aspects constitute one person. However, within this basic unity there is a tri-dimensionality, because a human being is self conscious, world conscious, and God-conscious. He can look inward, outward, and upward. But he is, nonetheless, one person, with one individual human nature.[3]

The holistic trichotomist would agree with Geisler's description of man's makeup.

The emphasis on the fundamental *unity* of man's personhood differs from some proponents of classical trichotomy. The statement, "Man is a spirit, who has a soul and lives in a body" would be a compartmentalized model, not the holistic model advocated here. In an article warning against negative tendencies, Brian Onken documented examples of those who use the soul/spirit distinction to denigrate the faculty of mind and emotions:

> Seeing that the intellectual capacities are relegated to a place in the soul, and seeing that the spirit is viewed as the component of man which he communicates with God, it is possible that this view could result in a denigration of the intellect and a degrading of the value of doctrine or theology (viewed as a function of the intellect) in the Christian life.[4]

Onken admits that this problem is not automatically caused by trichotomy, yet he does quote examples of this anti-intellectual attitude by trichotomous writers. *Holistic* trichotomy would heed this warning and affirm that loving God with one's mind (and verifying all doctrine by the Word of God) is in harmony with man's inner makeup.

If the admission of only two separable elements in man seems to allow the dichotomist to deny the spirit's distinct existence, one should note than some evangelical dichotomists would rather be monist, the only impediment being the biblical data about the separation that occurs in physical death. Yet, Adam would have had both a material and immaterial substance even if death did not enter human history (causing the soul to separate from the body temporarily at death and proving this duality). Even so, the spirit can be distinct from the soul without having to prove this distinction by a separate, independent existence from it. Some regard this kind of distinction in the immaterial realm as an unnecessary refinement, yet such precision is scriptural. For example, in interpreting the indwelling of the Holy Spirit, one must discern that the Holy Spirit indwells the believer's immaterial part as "one [unified] spirit" (1 Cor 6:17) without deifying man. "The Spirit Himself bears witness with our spirit that we are children of God" (Rom 8:16). Both are "spirit," yet ontologically distinct.

The threefold makeup of man corresponds with many aspects of his design and role. Although these distinctions may overlap, consider the following contrasts. In regard to life, the body has biological life, the soul has personal life, and the (regenerated) spirit has eternal life (cf. the connotations of the New Testament vocabulary for life: *bios, psuche, and zoe*). In regard to aptitude, the body is fitted for the environment of earth, the soul is fitted for personal relationships, and the spirit is fitted for worship (John 4:23; Rom 12:11). In regard to spiritual gifts, the body can carry out the soul's decisions, and the soul can cooperate with the spirit (when endued with a gift). Paul indirectly confirms this distinction in his corrective remarks to the Corinthians: "For if I pray in a tongue, my spirit prays, but my understanding [mental faculty of the soul] is unfruitful" (1 Cor 14:14; cf. 14:2,15,16). In regard to awareness, the body is sense-conscious, the soul is self-conscious, and the (regenerated) spirit is God-conscious (1 Cor 2:14). In regard to organic qualities, the life of the body is distinct from inorganic matter, the life of the soul is distinct from the life of plants (depending upon higher reason instead of instinct), and the life of the human spirit is distinct from animals (with higher reasoning and creativity instead of instinct).

In the soul and spirit there are a variety of functional attributes. These faculties involve both parts, but are primarily attributed to one or the other. Watchman Nee's extensive work is representative of the allocation of faculties to the soul and spirit among trichotomist writers. Nee identified the faculties of the soul as intellect, emotions and will. The spirit's faculties include intuition, communion, and conscience.[5]

What is the basis for assigning these faculties to their respective parts of soul and spirit? As a living being, the human soul has qualities that distinguish it from plant life. Higher forms of animal life also have these higher-than-plant life faculties. For example, plants do not have a conscious intellect, emotions, or will, whereas a horse, dog, cat, etc., noticeably has each of these. (Farmers and pet owners could readily confirm this.)

To distinguish the faculties especially allocated to the human spirit, we take note of man's creation in God's image:

> Then God said, "Let Us make man in Our image, according to Our likeness; let them have dominion over the fish of the sea, over the birds of the air, and over the cattle, over all the earth and over every creeping thing that creeps on the earth." So God created man in His own image; in the image of God He created him; male and female He created them (Gen 1:26,27).

In order to clarify which faculties in us are attributed to the human spirit (rather than the soul) we need to discern which faculties we have that are above those of animals. (Whereas the secular humanist would reduce man as the highest form of evolved, animal life, believers should accept the scriptural testimony of our higher, distinctive, spiritual capacities.)

The spirit's faculties of intuition, conscience and communion can be confirmed by our inner experience and the testimony of the Bible. *Intuition* can be defined as man's ability to discern spiritual truth. Although this capacity is hindered in man after the Fall, enough functionality remains to render him responsible to positively respond to God's witness in nature (Rom 1:18-20). This functionality is restored through the new birth of the spirit:

Now we have received, not the spirit of the world, but the Spirit who is from God, that we might *know* the things that have been freely given to us by God. These things we also speak, not in words which man's wisdom teaches but which the Holy Spirit teaches, comparing spiritual things with spiritual. But the natural [soulical] *man does not receive the things of the Spirit of God,* for they are foolishness to him; *nor can he know them, because they are spiritually discerned*" (1 Cor 2:12-14).

Even with God's image damaged in fallen man, the faculty of *conscience* is still functioning and recognized in Scripture. "For when Gentiles, who do not have the law, by nature do the things in the law, these, although not having the law, are a law to themselves, who show the work of the law written in their hearts, their conscience also bearing witness, and between themselves their thoughts accusing or else excusing them" (Rom 2:14,15). Through regeneration the believer's sins have been pardoned. Now he is summoned to live in accordance to the testimony of his conscience (cf. Rom 14:20-24; 1 Tim 1:5).

Communion with God was the special privilege of Adam and Eve in the Garden of Eden. However, when sin entered, this relationship was broken, requiring God's redemptive work to reconcile them to Himself (Gen 2:16,17; 3:15,21). The unregenerate person has no personal fellowship with God, since this faculty (as the other spiritual capacities) was damaged by Adam's sin (Isa 59:1,2; Eph 2:1). In this condition there is an emptiness and spiritual void that only a personal relationship with God can fill. Communion with God is one step away—the step of receiving His salvation by repentance and faith. Believers have the restored privilege of full communion with God through the high priestly ministry of Christ: "Let us therefore come boldly to the throne of grace, that we may obtain mercy and find grace to help in time of need" (Heb 4:16). And Paul affirmed, "God is faithful, by whom you were called into the fellowship of His Son, Jesus Christ our Lord" (1 Cor 1:9). Thus, we see by personal experience, logical deduction, and the testimony of Scripture that the inner faculties that higher animals also possess are similar to man's soul, whereas faculties unique to man are assigned to the man's spirit.

Analogies of Holistic Trichotomy

God's Triunity

A theological parallel has been noted between the nature of the Trinity and man's triunity. God is one (Deut 6:4) yet with three "persons" (2 Cor 13:14). God the Father is a distinct person from God the Holy Spirit, yet both are spirit and neither has been clothed with human nature as the Son has. This parallel may be strengthened when man is considered as made in God's image (Gen 1:26,27). Although this similarity may not be a proof of man's triune nature, this parallel seems to be more than coincidental. As mentioned above, some have used this comparison as a significant argument in favor of trichotomy.[6] When St. Patrick ministered in Ireland, he used the common shamrock with its three petals to illustrate God's three-in-one nature. Missionaries to Muslims have used the illustration of the sun, which manifests heat, light, and time. Although illustrations can be helpful, they all have limitations. Likewise, these analogies of trichotomy, while imperfect, can serve to clarify and reinforce the spirit, soul, and body distinctions in man.

The Believer as the New Testament Tabernacle

The symbolism of the tabernacle's Holy Place and Holy of Holies can be a useful analogy in clarifying the kind of distinctions in man's makeup. What at first may be an unexpected comparison becomes more reasonable when one recalls the believer's role as a temple of the Holy Spirit (1 Cor 3:16; 6:19; Col 1:27). This analogy was mentioned in the previous chapter with quotations from Martin Luther. More recently, Ray Stedman likewise referred to the tabernacle as an intentional symbol for man's spirit, soul, and body. Commenting on Hebrews 9:11, he observed,

> In equating the human spirit with heaven, I do not mean to imply that the human spirit in which the Spirit of Christ dwells is equivalent with all that Scripture includes in the word *heaven*. I simply mean that there is an obvious correspondence between the two and that in the spirit we are

in some sense living in heaven now (Eph. 2:6). Moses saw, of course, the whole person—body, soul and spirit (Gen 2:7; 1 Thes 5:23). This would explain the threefold division of the tabernacle. The outer court corresponds to the body; the Holy Place, to the soul; and the Most Holy Place, to the spirit. Even the furniture of the tabernacle corresponds to elements in us. For instance, the furniture of the Holy Place was the lampstand, the table of bread, and the altar of incense. If the Holy Place is the soul of man, these pieces would suggest the mind (lampstand), the emotions (bread as a symbol of social intercourse) and the will (altar of incense, which reflects the choices God approves). But Moses was shown that though God dwells in the human spirit and makes us different from the animals, we have no access to him because of sin. We are described as "dead in trespasses and sins" and said to be "alienated from God," "without God in the world." But Paul states the great truth of Hebrews 9 in these words "But now in Christ Jesus you who once were far away have been brought near through the blood of Christ" (Eph 2:13).[7]

Stedman's notes are significant in light of his respected ministry as an expository biblical preacher and author.

The tabernacle had a courtyard with a fenced perimeter (like the physical body), and one structure for the ministry of the priests. *The question, "Is the immaterial side of man composed of one part or two?" may be compared to the question, "Was the tabernacle building one part or two?"* In a way, it was one building, distinct from the courtyard. Even so, the soul is often used in Scripture to denote the immaterial side of man. Yet, the tabernacle building was designed by God as having two parts. The Holy of Holies was distinct in being—not just conceptually—from the Holy Place. The Holy of Holies was only separated from the Holy Place by the curtain (a less obvious distinction than the entrance to the building from the courtyard). The Holy of Holies was unknown experientially, except for the high priest who entered it on the Day of Atonement. Likewise, the distinction of the spirit from the soul does not rest on empirical data; it rests on revelation. Even so, the distinction between soul and spirit is less evident than that of the distinction of body from soul.

Man As Spirit, Soul, and Body

To elaborate on this, holistic trichotomy differs from dichotomy by insisting on the ontological distinction between soul and spirit. The human spirit is more than that a particular function, attribute, role, or relationship of the soul; it is actually distinct from the soul proper. Returning to the analogy of the tabernacle, the Holy of Holies had properties, features, and roles that separated it from the Holy Place. The furniture was different, its accessibility was different (only the high priest could enter), its frequency of access was different (only on *Yom Kippur*), and its source of light was different (no lampstand as in the Holy Place). Even so, man's spirit is to be illuminated only by the Spirit of God, not by naturalistic inquiry through the physical senses (1 Cor 2:11-14).

It would be incorrect to surmise that the Holy Place was just the tabernacle thought of in relation to the priesthood, whereas the Holy of Holies was only the tabernacle thought of in connection with God's presence. These two terms were more than differing connotations; they were separate and distinguishable parts of the one building. Similarly, the "soul" is *not* (as dichotomists have asserted) just the immaterial part of man thought of in relation to his earthly relationships, whereas "spirit" is man's one immaterial part as thought of in relationship with God. Rather, in addition to the differing connotations, the soul and spirit denote distinguishable, distinct parts of man.

The Nation of Israel

The composite nature of the nation of Israel in the Old Testament is analogous to the soul/spirit distinction in man. After the revolt of the northern tribes during the reign of King Rehoboam, Israel became divided into two—Israel and Judah (1 Kings 12). In one sense they had a singular identity as God's covenant people. However, after 930 B.C., there were different kings (several ungodly dynasties in the north, but the Davidic dynasty in the south), different approaches to worship (the idolatrous shrines in the north, but the Temple of Jerusalem in the south), and different exiles (722 B.C. to Assyria in the north, but 586 B.C. to Babylon in the south). Similarly, the immaterial side of man is one, yet, the soul and spirit are distinct. And as the differences between the northern and southern kingdom increased through Ephraim's unfaithfulness, so the condition of man before and after regeneration gives further clarification of the distinct nature and functions of the human soul and spirit. In addition to biblical illustrations, we can consider some contemporary analogies.

The United States of America

Does the U.S.A. consist of one, two, three or more parts? Is this just semantics? Not at all. An accurate understanding of this nation's political and physical makeup is essential for a true knowledge of its identity, structure, geography, and history.

Like monism, the country has a singular identity as a democratic republic. There is one president, one flag, one nation. However, like the multifaceted view of man, the U.S.A. has divisions of states, counties, and cities. Since "States" is her middle name, an accurate knowledge of America will recognize fifty member states. However, some contexts require us to recognize some distinct features of the nation's physical makeup. Like a dichotomist, one could assert that America has two categories, the contiguous states and the non-contiguous states. Alaska and Hawaii have similarities: they both became states in 1959, and are separate from the forty eight that are south of Canada. When someone is approximating the location of the U.S.A., he/she would point to the heart of North America. However, in other contexts, accuracy would require acknowledgement of the two non-contiguous states.

As in trichotomy, the nation's physical map has three distinct parts: the contiguous states, Alaska, and Hawaii. To ignore these distinctions would create a major problem for the person seeking to drive the 2,300 miles west of California to visit Hawaii in the North Pacific Ocean! It is unmistakable that Alaska is distinct from Hawaii in location and governmental identity. Even Alaska's name demonstrates this; it is derived from *alaskax* and literally means "land that is not an island." A student of the U.S.A. that might think it unsophisticated to differentiate Alaska and Hawaii would obviously be in error. The makeup of the nation is a separate issue from what should be emphasized and how America should be discussed.

Three Parts of an Egg

When I was a student in Bible college, I had a part time job delivering eggs. My employer was a poultry farmer who had several delivery routes. Having delivered countless dozens of these, an analogy came to mind. In a sense an egg is one. (Take away the shell or insides and it would be considered incomplete.) This observation is similar to *monism*. However, considered as a vehicle for the hatching of a chicken, an egg is recognized as having two parts (the shell and the chick). This is similar to *dichotomy*. However, when eggs are used in cooking, there is an ontological distinction in the inner volume of an egg. A baking recipe sometimes calls for egg whites or egg yokes. These are visible, actual parts of the egg.

This organic distinction is more than conceptual. The egg white is not the egg when considered as food with the yoke only an egg when considered as a potential chick. Similarly, the soul and spirit are actually distinct, not just different terms for two functions/connotations of the immaterial side of man.

Context is a key issue in sorting out "parts." How the parts of an egg are differentiated relates to the context of the egg's use. As a vocabulary word, "egg" is singular. As a chick breaks out of its shell, there are clearly two parts—the shell and the chick. However, in baking, the distinction between egg whites and egg yokes is more than semantics. Likewise, in some contexts monism or dichotomy can be functionally adequate models. However, when dealing with the doctrines of regeneration and sanctification, for example, the distinction of soul and spirit is more than semantics.

The Spirit as an "Organ" of the Soul

The task of defining the distinction of spirit from soul requires theological precision and exegetical sensitivity; concrete terms are used for abstract concepts. A term that may be useful in clarifying the spirit's distinction from the soul is "organ" (as "in" an organ of the body). Just as the body has a plurality of organs, yet is one organism, so the soul has a distinct organ, i.e., the spirit. The biblical data support the distinctive usage of spirit as it relates to man's makeup.

As an organ has a particular, distinct function in the organism, so the spirit has a distinctive function with the soul. The spirit is the organ that "died" at the Fall, and is regenerated at conversion. To enhance this analogy, this organ can be compared to the physical eye, serving the soul as a "lamp": "The spirit of a man is the lamp of the LORD, Searching all the inner depths of his heart" (Prov 20:27). This parallel is illustrated in Christ's warning of the use of the eyes: "The lamp of the body is the eye. Therefore, when your eye is good, your whole body also is full of light. But when your eye is bad, your body also is full of darkness" (Luke 11:34). Similarly, if the human spirit is unregenerate, the mind has no true, personal knowledge of God. The Holy Spirit is the One Who regenerates and sanctifies the believer; the human spirit is the primary locus of that illumination.

The Human Brain

Another analogy that may facilitate a scriptural conception of the distinction of soul and spirit in a holistic context is the design of the human brain. The human brain is one unit, with the cerebrum divided into halves—the left cerebral hemisphere and the right cerebral hemisphere. Researchers have assigned distinct types of reasoning processes to each hemisphere. However, the dynamics of right and left hemispheres of the human brain are not merely different types of reasoning; they are biologically distinct. Even so, man has one immaterial element, yet this is composed of two parts (hemispheres), similar to the physical distinction of the right and left parts of the brain.

Summary

Defining this model does not remove the mystery of the inner workings of the immaterial part of man. Dichotomists affirm that there remains a mystery in how the body and soul interact. Berkhof confessed, "Body and soul are distinct substances, which do interact, though the mode of their interaction remains a mystery for us."[8] How much more should theologians use sensitivity and patience in debating the finer distinctions of the soul and spirit. Holistic trichotomy retains

Man As Spirit, Soul, and Body

the Old Testament perspective on the essential unity of the human person, while fully accepting the more detailed, distinctive identification of the human spirit as revealed in the New Testament epistles. It also recognizes the two fundamental aspects of man's existence: material and immaterial. However, holistic trichotomy refuses to view the spirit and soul as mere synonyms of the same ontological part of man. This chapter has sought to define and illustrate the two parts of man's immaterial side—soul and spirit.

Several analogies have been considered in the quest to confirm and clarify holistic trichotomy. The human spirit can be compared to an organ of the soul, the Holy of Holies in the tabernacle, or a distinct "hemisphere" of the human brain. Whether considering the lofty concept of the triune nature of God, or common examples such as the composition of the U.S.A., or a chicken egg, each analogy offers some idea about grasping holistic trichotomy. They do not prove this model, but illustrate the two parts of man's immaterial nature—soul and spirit.

Holistic trichotomy should be more palatable to dichotomists, for only two parts of man are said to be separable. We do well to keep in mind that words/names are linguistic tools to help people understand reality. If the concepts of the distinction of soul and spirit—as defined and proposed here—are accepted, the *name* of the model (*holistic trichotomy*) is secondary. If the other two positions dare not change their basic orientation, they could pick more acceptable nomenclature. (Those who emphasize the unity of man could acknowledge the soul and spirit distinction with a designation like "complex monism." Those who emphasize duality, yet concede the soul and spirit distinction, might use a designation such as "distinctive dichotomy."

The main task for biblical psychology, however, is the articulation of scriptural definitions of man's constituent parts and their related faculties. The goal of this chapter has been to affirm insights about man's makeup that do not go beyond what is written, but to express accurately the implications of New Testament revelation on the subject. The next chapter will seek to validate the preceding conclusions by responding to some traditional objections.

[1] Clark, *The Biblical Doctrine of Man*, 33.

[2] Norman Geisler, *Systematic Theology* (Minneapolis, MN: Bethany House, 2003), 2:452.

[3] Ibid, 2:452.

[4] Brian Onken, *Dangers of the 'Trinity'* in Man (Christian Research Institute), 2. One should balance his warning against the opposite danger. For example, proponents of liberal, rationalistic, and neoorthodox "theology" put the independent mind in ascendancy over proper spiritual intuition. The spirit's intuition in man should be directed by the Holy Spirit-inspired Scriptures (1 Cor 2:14; 2 Tim 3:16) and govern the mind's conclusions with revealed truth: "casting down arguments and every high thing that exalts itself against the knowledge of God, bringing every thought into captivity to the obedience of Christ" (2 Cor 10:5).

[5] Nee, *The Spiritual Man*, 1:31-38.

[6] Ed Bulkley, *Why Christians Can't Trust Psychology*, 339. Cf. Mal Couch, *The Doctrine of God*, ch. 6, www.ConservativeOnline.org.

[7] Ray C. Stedman, *Hebrews* (Illinois: InterVarsity Press, 1992), 97. Note also Stedman's application of trichotomy in the temptations of Christ narrative in *Adventuring through the Bible* (Grand Rapids, Discovery House Publishers, 1997) 494; Cf. *Understanding Man* (Portland: Multnomah 1975) 25,26. Adrian Rogers also saw in the tabernacle a symbol of man as spirit, soul, and body: *The Power of His Presence* (Wheaton: Crossway Books, 1995) 17-20. Cf. Clarence Larken, *Dispensational Truth or God's Plan and Purpose in the Ages* (1918), 97.

[8] Berkhof, *Systematic Theology*, 195.

Chapter 7
Defending Trichotomy

Responses to Objections

Before concluding the main section of this book, the question needs to be faced: Are the arguments against trichotomy unanswerable? Although some of these challenges have been indirectly addressed in previous chapters, here we will consider additional responses to criticisms against traditional trichotomy. Below is a basic list of challenges followed by a brief response for each.

Interchangeability of Terms

The first objection to be considered is the claim that Scripture uses "soul" and "spirit" interchangeably. This is the primary objection to trichotomy by most evangelical dichotomists. It is thought that the significant overlap in these terms requires the interpretation that they are only synonyms of man's immaterial part. That "soul" and "spirit" share many meanings is readily conceded; (see Part 1, chapter 3.) We concede that in the Old Testament the distinction between these parts of man terms can be supported, but not proven. *This early ambiguity is due to the nature of progressive revelation.* The obvious distinction between body and soul is not explicit in the concrete style of Hebrew thought and language; therefore, we need not expect a definitive case for the subtle distinctions between the soul and spirit in the Old Testament. If this admission seems to jeopardize the proposition of trichotomy, consider Berkhof's comment about the lack of decisive evidence for dichotomy in the Old Testament alone:

We should be careful, however, not to expect the latter distinction between the body as the material element, and the soul as the spiritual element of human nature, in the Old Testament. This antithesis—soul and body—even in its New Testament sense, is not yet found in the Old Testament.[1]

The personal nature of the Holy Spirit as a member of the triune Godhead was not explicitly revealed in the Old Testament either; it should not be surprising that the distinctive role of the human spirit would require New Testament revelation as well.

There are several examples of the similar usage of soul and spirit in the New Testament that are used as evidence against trichotomy. Both soul and spirit can be troubled (John 12:27; 13:21); they both can be involved in worship (Luke 1:46,47); they both can be objects of salvation (Jas 1:21; 1 Cor 5:5); they both are involved in thinking (Acts 14:2; 1 Cor 2:11); and they both are used with "body" to describe the whole person (Matt 10:28; Jas 2:6). These and other examples are given to prove that the terms are used interchangeably. These examples only document that the terms have a significant overlap. Often a biblical writer conveys his point by using either term, with the appropriate connotation. This overlap of meanings does not dictate that the soul and spirit are just synonyms for man's immaterial side.

That overlapping terms do not prove non-distinction of soul and spirit is illustrated by the following observations: (a) The Hebrew term, *Nephesh* [soul], is sometimes used to describe a dead body, yet this does not prove that the soul and body are not distinct parts of man (Num 6:6; Lev 24:18); (b) The *Spirit* of Christ and the Holy *Spirit* are both titles of the third person of the Trinity, but this does not equate the Son and the Spirit (Rom 8:11; 1 Cor 3:16); (c) Both animals and humans have *nephesh*, but this does not invalidate man's distinctive quality of soul which is necessitated by his creation in God's image (Gen 1:24; 2:19). Even so, overlap in word usage does not prove soul and spirit to be mere synonyms of one immaterial part of man.

The use of *sheol* demonstrates the way an Old Testament Hebrew term has a scope of meaning that requires later revelation to clarify doctrinally. The King James Version translates sheol thirty one times as "grave," thirty one times as "hell," and three times as "pit." The concrete style of this language associates a whole in the ground with a pit that someone may fall into, a place to bury someone, and the destiny of a person after this mortal life. Later revelation in the Bible indicates that the grave is not the end of man's existence. Heaven and hell are destinations of the soul/spirit after physical death (1 Pet 1:4; Matt 25:46). There will also be a bodily resurrection (Rev. 20:12-14). Similarly, *nephesh* and *ruach* can have overlapping usage in the Old Testament without this requiring them to be names of the same part in man. Later revelation clarifies their features as distinguishable parts of a person.

Another example used in the dichotomist case for the interchangeability of these terms is their use as relating to salvation. The soul is saved (Heb 10:39) and the spirit is saved (1 Cor 5:5). Although this could be explained as another example of synecdoche, it may point to a more detailed model of salvation in the epistles. The body of a converted person is not credited with "redemption" until the resurrection; believers are "...eagerly waiting for the adoption, the redemption of our body" (Rom 8:23). On the other hand, salvation is described as an accomplished fact for the one who is regenerated (Eph 2:1-8); the believer's spirit is one with God's Spirit (1 Cor 6:17), Who "Himself bears witness with our spirit that we are children of God" (Rom 8:16). This indicates that the soul is presently in the process of being saved (Jas 1:21: Ps 23:3). Thus, technically, the believer's spirit is *already saved* from the penalty of sin; his soul is *being saved* from the power of sin, and his body *will be saved* from the presence of sin at the resurrection (Phil 3:20,21). The New Testament confirms the need for the functional attributes of the believer's soul to be progressively delivered from the influence of sin. The mind is to be renewed (Rom 12:2), the will is to be yielded (Luke 9:23), and the emotions are to be directed (Phil 4:4). Thus, the three aspects of salvation correlate with the parts of man.

In listing arguments against trichotomy, Wayne Grudem mentions the unity of man by describing the involvement of the body in virtually every activity of the soul.

> We should not slip into the mistake of thinking that certain activities (such as thinking, feeling, or deciding things) are done by only one part of us. Rather, these activities are done by the whole person. When we think or feel things,

certainly our physical bodies are involved in every point as well.[3]

Grudem's observation is a valid one. Yet, if the dichotomist affirms that every action involves both/all parts of a person's makeup, he should not object to the trichotomist's view that, as an distinct organ of the soul, the spirit is expressed through it. On the other hand, his criterion of requiring a function of the soul to always have a counterpart in the physical organism could be used as an argument for monism (which Grudem rejects).

By synecdoche, the spirit can be used of the soul and often is (1 Cor 16:18; 2 Tim 4:22). This does not negate the distinction between them; the context determines the usage intended. As was shown in the chapter on word studies, several lexicons support the distinction of spirit from soul as more than one of connotation (e.g., Cremer, Thayer, Vines, and TWBOT). Similarly, the soul is often used to represent the whole person (although dichotomists concede that man is body *and* soul).

One of the distinctive qualities of the regenerated human spirit is that it is essentially holy—a partaker of God's nature (2 Pet 1:4; 1 Cor 1:2; 6:17). Therefore, Paul can testify that he delights in the law of God in the inner man (Rom 7:22). An objection has been raised to this trichotomous interpretation. 2 Corinthians 7:1 seems to indicate that the spirit can prompt sin: "Therefore, having these promises, beloved, let us cleanse ourselves from all filthiness of the flesh and *spirit*, perfecting holiness in the fear of God." This has been interpreted as referring to intrinsic sinfulness in the believer's spirit. The concept of total depravity tends to assume the redeemed spirit is still sinful by nature.

In response, the trichotomist reaffirms the basic unity of man's personhood. Although the spirit is the part that primarily expresses God's life in the believer, this never removes responsibility from the spirit. Man is unified in personhood and responsibility. Then, what is the precise nature of the spirit's need for "cleansing" in 2 Corinthians 7:1? The previous context gives a clue, describing the need for consecration. This practice alludes to the holiness concepts of the Old Testament. One of those concepts is the danger of defilement with unholy things, even if the Israelites were holy as God's people (Lev 21:1-14). Similarly, the believer must guard against the defilement of

Man As Spirit, Soul, and Body

worldly values and demonic influences—both of which can still be understood as technically external to his/her spirit (Rom 12:2; Eph 6:10). Another indication that this cleansing from filthiness does not pertain essentially to the human spirit's nature is that *pneuma* in this verse does not have the definite article in Greek. Thus, Paul is warning against referring to spiritual sins (e.g., pride, unbelief) as well as sensual ones (e.g., lust, gluttony).

Another way the usage of spirit is distinct from the soul is that "spirit" usually describes the believer after physical death, although both soul and spirit stay together (Acts 23:8,9; Heb 12:23). This usage corresponds with what one would expect of man's spirit in its primary relationship to God. The only New Testament exceptions (to referring to the intermediate state in terms of "soul") occur in Rev 6:9 and 20:4. In these passages the context is martyrdom; this shifts the emphasis to the *bodily release* of the immaterial part of man at death.

There are other distinctions in the New Testament usage of "spirit." Beckwith and Oehler mention several: (a) the spirit does not die nor is it killed; (b) the spirit is not the subject of inclination, or aversion; (c) whatever belongs to the spirit belongs to the soul also, but not everything that belongs to the soul belongs to the spirit as well (cf. the tabernacle analogy).[4] Oehler further observed that the soul is used of the subject as personal and individual, but the spirit is not so used. Drawing on Genesis 2:17 and Job 33:4 he specified that the soul exists and lives only by the vitalizing power of the spirit.[5]

In his extensive word study on *pneuma,* Eduard Schweiser noted that *pneuma* is always used to contrast *sarx* [flesh] in the unbeliever, never *psuche*; *pneuma* is never used of non-Christians for impulses that are ethically negative; and it cannot be hated or persecuted as the soul can.[6] Kerr observed that spirit does not hunger or thirst, although these physical functions are sometimes attributed to the soul. Some have noted that God is the "Father of spirits," but never as the "Father of souls" (Heb 12:9; Zech 12:1). So, even though "soul" and "spirit" have an overlap in meaning, there are aspects of usage that differentiate them. If examples of synonymous usage disprove man's triunity, then the same methodology could be wrongfully employed to disprove God's triunity. The observations in previous chapters have given further evidence of the distinction between soul and spirit.

Terms Used in the Great Commandment

Another objection made against trichotomy is this: If 1 Thessalonians 5:23 is interpreted as referring to trichotomy, then the Great Commandment teaches that man has four parts. In the synoptic Gospels Christ identified the greatest commandment by quoting Deuteronomy 6:5: "You shall love the LORD your God with all your heart, with all your soul, and with all your strength" (cf. Lev 19:18; Matt 22:37; Mark 12:30; Luke 10:27). In the Gospels, "mind" is also included in this Great Commandment. In Matthew the preposition *en* is used to bring out the concept of instrumentality; (perhaps this is why he inserts "mind" but leaves out "strength"). The trichotomist sees the heart as including soul and spirit; the soul includes the mind; strength implies physical energy. The preposition used in Mark, *(ek)*, denotes inwardness. The aspects of man from Deuteronomy plus "mind" are used for emphasis.[7]

How does this differ from other texts used to show the ontological distinction between soul and spirit? First, the concrete style of the Old Testament language should be noted. Although the Gospel references are New Testament material, the quoted revelation is Mosaic. This source reflects its less precise articulation of man's inward parts. (See the comments on progressive revelation in chapter 4, footnote 2.) Waltke noted that the unifying emphasis of the "heart, soul, and might" rather than signifying different spheres of biblical psychology seem to be semantically concentric. They were chosen to reinforce the absolute singularity of personal devotion to God.[8]

Either Deuteronomy 6:5 and parallels are used as demonstrating a multifaceted model of man, or 1 Thessalonians (and related verses examined in chapters 2-6) function as definitive on man's makeup. Paul's intention in 1 Thessalonians 5:23 is to specify the different aspects of man that should be entirely sanctified. "Now may the God of peace Himself sanctify you completely; and may your whole *spirit, soul, and body* be preserved blameless at the coming of our Lord Jesus Christ."

The importance of progressive revelation is crucial here as well. Paul's epistles give further clarity about the subtle differences between soul and spirit. This New Testament epistle should be expected to give more advanced light on the immaterial parts of man than the Mosaic quotation of the Great Commandment. *1 Thessalonians 5:23 is not used as an isolated proof text; rather, it is a uniquely important declaration due to its place in the Bible's progressive revelation.*

In his exposition of 1 Thessalonians 5:23, Robert Thomas demonstrated that non-trichotomous renderings of this verse do not do justice to its meaning. This extended quote presents a scholarly summary in favor of this definitive interpretation:

> That Paul saw man as a threefold substance in this verse [v. 23] has been generally recognized since the early fathers. The symmetrical arrangement of three nouns with their articles and their connection by means of two "ands" (*kai*) renders this the most natural explanation. This becomes a "distinct enunciation of three component parts of the nature of man" (Ellicott, p. 84). That Paul elsewhere does not make such a distinction (Best, pp. 242-244; Hendriksen, pp. 146,147) is no argument against trichotomy. It is always possible that Paul has been misunderstood elsewhere. It is also conceivable that he did not endeavor to make specific distinctions in other letters as he does here. That Paul possibly depends on liturgical formulation and attaches no special meaning to these separate terms (Dibelius, cited by Best, p. 244) is also inconclusive speculation. To object that this interpretation reads in the trichotomy of secular psychology (Schweizer, TDNT, 6:435) neglects Paul's occasional acceptance of portions of secular philosophy that were valid. He simply incorporated them into a divinely inspired framework (Ellicott, p. 84). A trichotomous understanding of 5:23 has so much to commend it that other interpretations cannot compete without summoning arguments from elsewhere. The difference between the material part ("body") and the immaterial parts ("spirit" and "soul") is obvious. Paul's pronounced distinction between *psychikos* ("natural"; NIV, "without the spirit") and *pneumatikos* ("spiritual") (1 Cor 2:14, 15; 15:44), his differentiation of *pneuma* ("spirit") and ego ("self") or nous ("mind"), parts of psyche ("soul") (Rom 7:17-23; 1 Cor 14:14), and other writers' distinguishing of *pneuma* and *psyche* (James 3:15; Jude 19) argue heavily for a substantial, not just a functional, difference between the two immaterial parts (Hiebert, p. 252; Schweizer, TDNT, 6:436; Lightfoot, p. 88).

The spirit (*pneuma*) is the part that enables man to perceive the divine. Through this component he can know and communicate with God. This higher element, though damaged through the fall of Adam, is sufficiently intact to provide each individual a consciousness of God. The soul (*psyche*) is the sphere of man's will and emotions. Here is his true center of personality. It gives him a self-consciousness that relates to the physical world through the body and to God through the spirit. This analysis of man had been Paul's training in the O. T., and no impressive evidence has surfaced to eradicate such a picture here (Milligan, p. 78; Olshausen, p. 457). Yet, it must be confessed, much unresolved mystery remains regarding the interrelationships between man's different parts, including the body. How one affects the other is fully understood only by him who is the Creator. For such a composite creature Paul therefore prays, seeking an unblamable wholeness in the presence "of our Lord Jesus Christ" (23; cf. 1 Thes 2:19; 3:13).[9]

Therefore, the trichotomy of 1 Thessalonians 5:23 should regulate how the psychological terms in the Great Commandment are discerned.

Alleged Contradictions

It has been asserted that passages interpreted in support of trichotomy would necessarily contradict any that teach two parts of man.[10] This argument assumes that trichotomy is of a crude model that contradicts descriptions of the person as essentially twofold—material and immaterial.

This charge can be answered with this observation: there is variation in scriptural testimony, but not contradiction. Since the spirit is not separated from the soul, a summary statement that only mentions two parts of a person does not contradict ones that clarify the third part. *Passages that distinguish spirit from soul are presenting further detail and precision.* A similar explanation is required to avoid other apparent discrepancies in Scripture. Examples of this principle of variance without contradiction can be found in the Gospels. Were there two angels at Christ's empty tomb (Luke 24:4) or one (Matt 28:2)? Were there two demoniacs in Gadera (Matt 8:28) or one (Mark 5:2)?

Man As Spirit, Soul, and Body

Where there two blind men healed at Jericho (Matt 20:30) or just Bartimaeus (Mark 10:46)? In each case, one writer gives less detail than the other. These differences in quantity of information do not indicate contradictions in Scripture. Similarly, texts that present man as body and soul do not contradict others that present the added detail of body, soul, and spirit.

The Role of Conscious Awareness

The objection has been made that the Bible is ambiguous on whether man has two or three parts so the matter should be judged on rational grounds, which favors dichotomy.[11] The rational grounds are said to favor dichotomy because of a lack of a conscious awareness of the spirit.[12] There are several problems with this line of reasoning. First, this argument applied to anatomy would doubt the existence of the immaterial part of man that is not biologically verifiable. Thus, materialism sees man as restricted to the material realm. Since man is created by God in His image, the question of the parts of man's immaterial side must be decided on a different basis. Evidence has been presented above for interpreting spirit as the organ of God-consciousness, and the soul as the organ of self-consciousness. Likewise, Romans chapters 6-8 present the detailed description of the conscious, internal struggle of the believer with his physical members (of the body), the flesh and the will (of the soul), and the law of God in the inner man (the spirit). *Therefore, biblical revelation and the experiential dynamics of one's internal struggle can be better explained through a trichotomous model.*
Even without the biblical testimony, conscious awareness could just as readily indicate a soul/spirit distinction. There is a higher reasoning and awareness that sets humans above animals. This could be explained by the presence of the human spirit. The phenomenon of one's internal self talk/conversation —and even a distinct evaluative stance—could also indicate the soul/spirit distinction in man.

The Use of "Soul" in Relation to God

This argument against trichotomy is that, since "soul" is ascribed to God, therefore He can relate directly to man's soul; the organ of spirit in man is unnecessary.[13] One could challenge the proposition that God has a soul in a way similar to man's soul. *Although the word "soul" is used in relation to God (Jer 5:9; 6:8) this usage is rare and should be interpreted anthropomorphically.* Similarly, God is said to have a hand, back, eyes, a right arm, etc., yet theologians do not deduce from these statements that God has a physical body (prior to the incarnation of the Son). Rather, His essential nature is spirit: "God is *Spirit*, and those who worship Him must worship in *spirit* and truth" (John 4:24). Therefore, God is essentially invisible (1 Tim 1:17). Granted, God is a personal being Who has made man in His image. He does have faculties of mind, will, and emotions (which are functional attributes of the human soul); yet the application of redemption is primarily the role of the Holy *Spirit* (Titus 3:5,6; 1 Cor 6:17). "The Spirit Himself bears witness with our *spirit* that we are children of God" (Rom 8:16). The twenty six New Testament occurrences of the adjective, "spiritual" (*pneumatikos*), as consistently positive and Godward, confirm the scriptural evidence for man's spirit as the primary organ for communion with the Holy Spirit.

The Tendency of Heretical Deviation

A further reason for the avoidance of trichotomy for some is the opinion that it is prone to heretical views. On the other hand, dichotomy is said to be a safeguard against doctrinal errors. It has been shown in chapter five that the heresy of Apollinaris brought trichotomy into disrepute; it is still recovering from this stigma. The Western Church found it easier to apply Occam's razor and take the simpler view, i.e., that man has only two parts. Strong is forthright in preferring dichotomy in order to refute automatically the following errors:

(a) That of the Gnostics, who held that the *pneuma* is part of the divine essence, and therefore incapable of sin. (b) That of the Appolinarians, who taught that Christ's humanity embraced only *soma* and *psuche*, while his divine nature furnished the *pneuma*. (c) That of the Semi-Pelagians, who excepted the human *pneuma* from the dominion of original sin. (d) That of Placeus, who held that only the *pneuma* was directly created by God. (e) That of Julius Muller, who held that the *psuche* comes to us from Adam, but that our *pneu-*

ma was corrupted in a previous state of being. (f) That of the Annihilationists, who hold that man at his creation had a divine element breathed into him, which he lost by sin, and which he recovers only at regeneration; so that only when he has this *pneuma* restored by virtue of his union with Christ does man become immortal, death being to the sinner a complete extinction of being.[14]

Admittedly, dichotomists have the convenience of refuting these kind of errors *a priori* due to eliminating the spirit as a distinct part of man. However, holistic trichotomy as presented in this book would also condemn the heretical views just listed. It should also be noted that heretical views also arise from monistic, and dichotomist models of man.[15]

This criticism of trichotomy is more a statement of preference than of veracity; it uses guilt by association. An example from church history can illustrate the problem inherent in this approach. During the Reformation, the Anabaptist movement grew out of a commitment to evaluate traditional beliefs in the light of Scripture. Infant baptism was rejected in favor of believer's baptism. However, the movement was quite divided; and there were extreme views and practices such as in the Munster revolt of 1534. John Matthys, an Anabaptist preacher, claimed himself Enoch, who would prepare for Christ's return. His group took over this German town, proclaiming it the New Jerusalem. They enforced community-of-goods and allowed polygamy. This episode affected the doctrinal preferences of the Lutherans. Walker noted, "Such fanaticism was popularly supposed to be characteristic of the Anabaptists, and the name became one of ignominy."[16] This was unfortunate, because the distinctives of believer's baptism, an eagerness for the Second Advent, and the separation of church and state should have been judged by the Bible alone, not by aberrations. *Likewise, heresies that incidentally have misrepresented the human spirit should not disqualify trichotomy.*

Summary

Much of the criticism directed toward the distinction of spirit, soul, and body, is side-stepped when the spirit is not defined as a separable part of man that has a different substance than that of the soul. We do not slight the academic credentials or sincerity of evangelical dichotomist theologians. Hopefully, readers will also notice the many respected voices cited in this book that advocate trichotomy. The case for holistic trichotomy would be further strengthened were it not for the frequent ambiguity in the Bible regarding spirit (as referring to either God's or man's). The responses above seek to demonstrate that trichotomy is based upon sound hermeneutics and is logically coherent. Although the objections mentioned above are not exhaustive, this chapter represents the defensibility of man as spirit, soul, and body. The concluding chapter will present some practical implications of this model of man in biblical counseling.

[1] Berkhof, *Systematic Theology*, 193.

[2] Grudem, *Systematic Theology*, 476.

[3] Beckwith, [NSHERK] *Biblical Conceptions of Soul and Spirit*, 12.

[4] Gustav F. Oehler, *Theology of the Old Testament* (NY: Funk and Wagnalls, 1883), 152.

[5] Ibid., 150.

[6] Gerhard Kittel and Gerhard Friedrich, eds., *Theological Dictionary of the New Testament* [TDNT] (Grand Rapids: Eerdmans, 1964) s.v. "Psuche," by Eduard Schweizer, 6: 649, 654-55.

[7] Eduard Schweizer, "Psuche," [TDNT], 6: 641.

[8] Bruce Waltke [TWBOT], s.v. "Nephesh," 2: 589.

[9] Robert Thomas, *1 Thessalonians*, in *The Expositor's Bible Commentary*, Frank Gaebelien, ed. (Zondervan, 1996), 69.

[10] Berkhof, *Systematic Theology*, 195.

[11] Henry C. Sheldon, *System of Christian Doctrine* (Boston: Carl H. Heintzemann, 1900), 274.

[12] Berkhof, *Systematic Theology*, 194. However, others have appealed to inner consciousness as an evidence of trichotomy (Van Osterzee, *Church Dogmatics*, 366. Some have considered that Freud's designation of id, ego and superego inadvertently parallel the bodily drives, the soul, and the spirit.

[13] Strong, *Systematic Theology*, 485.

[14] Strong, *Systematic Theology*, 487.

[15] For a survey of liberal and neo-orthodox views of the nature and functions of soul and spirit in man, see Agnes Sutherland, *The Spiritual Dimensions of Personality* (Philadelphia: Westminster Press, 1965).

[16] Walker, *A History of the Christian Church*, 336.

Man As Spirit, Soul, and Body

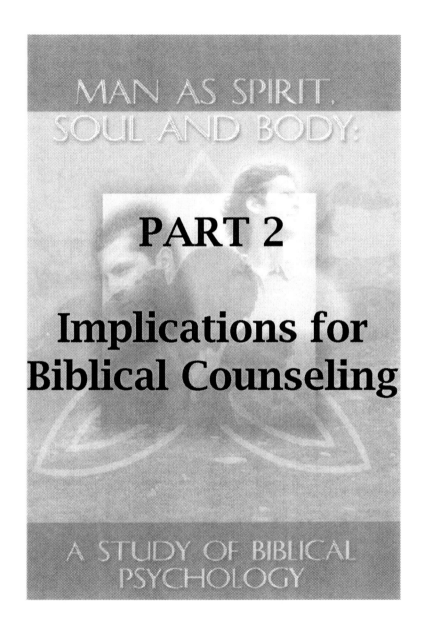

PART 2

Implications for Biblical Counseling

A STUDY OF BIBLICAL PSYCHOLOGY

Man As Spirit, Soul, and Body

Chapter 8
The Significance of Trichotomy in Biblical Counseling

The Centrality of the Bible in Christian Counseling

There has been a tendency in Christian counseling to water down the provision God has made for people's spiritual, mental, emotional, volitional, and physical needs. In his book, *The Sufficiency of Christ,* John MacArthur laments the shift toward psychology and away from the Bible's answers.

> I have no quarrel with those who use either common sense or social sciences as a helpful observer's platform to look on human conduct and develop tools to assist people in getting some external controls in their behavior. That may be useful as a first step for getting to the real spiritual cure. But a wise counselor realizes that all behavioral therapy stops on the surface—far short of actual solutions to the real needs of the soul, which are only resolved in Christ.[1]

There is a need for a Christian counseling models that go beyond an eclectic approach that is merely supplemented with the Bible.

In a standard secular text on counseling, Gerald Corey surveyed the major counseling models. He noted the need for clarifying one's philosophy and assumptions regarding counseling.

> It is my conviction that our views of human nature and the basic assumptions that undergird our views of the therapeutic process have significant implications for the way we develop our therapeutic practices. I am also persuaded that, because they do not pay sufficient attention to their philosophical assumptions, many practitioners operate

as though they had no set of assumptions regarding their clients. In my opinion, a central task is to make our assumptions explicit and conscious, so that we can establish some consistency between our beliefs about human nature and the way we implement our procedures in counseling or therapy."[2]

Without God's revelation to clarify the spiritual needs of man and give moral values and ethical absolutes, choosing a counseling model becomes very subjective. This being the case, it should not surprise the evangelical pastor that his counseling model should differ essentially from secular approaches.

Seminary professor, Jay Adams, wrote *Competent to Counsel* to make a case for the primacy of the Bible in equipping the pastoral counselor. He denounced the trend in Christian counseling of compromising with secular psychology. Adams contrasted the eclectic approach with the adequacy of the Bible. In *The Christian Counselor's Manual* he stated,

The eclectic pragmatically attempts to take the best of everything and glue it together in a patchwork. That we may not do as Christians, because instead of saying that nobody has anything (ultimate truth), we must say God has given us everything. This is the distinctive fact about the divine knowledge approach. The Scriptures plainly declare: "His divine power has given us everything we need for life and Godliness" (2 Pet 1:3).[3]

The Relevance of Biblical Psychology/Anthropology in Counseling

The study of the model of man is an important aspect of theology, yet its value is not limited to obtaining accurate belief. All theology relates to Christian living, and all Christian living should be anchored upon scriptural theology. In discussing the role of a theology of personal ministry, Lawrence Richards calls the theologian to apply doctrine to life.

Theology should not be a treatment of [mere] abstract ideas...theology must deal with reality...The theologian is called...[to] struggle with the ways in which what the Scriptures reveal finds expression in the life of the individual and the Christian community.[4]

Some Christian psychiatrists have affirmed the relevance of the Christian view of man in their approach to counseling. For example, O. Quentin Hyder stated,

For the committed Christian there is an additional dimension [to mental/physical health]. To him God is the ultimate reality, and spiritual and psychological health is to be in contact with that reality.[5]

Likewise, Jeffrey Boyd's research has validated the need to understand the patient as more than a monistic entity. He observed,

In secular American culture the vitality of life arises from our bodies, and if we would be spiritually healthy then we should exercise regularly, remain trim, eat little cholesterol, and wear Nike sneakers...But physical monism comes with a price: those who are suffering are plunged into worse suffering because they can no longer achieve the minimal requirements of being human—namely, having a vigorous and reliable body that is full of stamina, zest, sexiness and youth...Patients frequently tell me that when they lost their health they lost the meaning of life.[6]

The Christian view of man is not only scriptural, it promotes a useful, therapeutic model of counseling.

One purpose of this book is to validate trichotomy biblically, theologically, and historically, thereby endorsing deeper life sanctification in counseling. In his commentary on 1 Thessalonians, Lenski observed,

The [human] spirit ought to rule supreme; wholly controlled by God's Spirit, man ought to be *pneumatikos*. Sin enabled the *psuche* to control so that man became *psuchikos*, his bodily appetites having sway...*Modern psychology disregards it* [the trichotomous perspective] despite its supreme importance.[7]

In their book advocating the supremacy of the Bible in giving counsel, Martin and Deidre Bobgan refer to the role of the human spirit and sanctification which have been overlooked in secular counseling.

> One major limitation to psychotherapy is that it rarely, if ever, deals with the spiritual aspect of man. Its main sphere of concentration is with the mind, will and emotions...Sanctification, on the other hand, deals with the whole man, which includes the body, soul, and spirit...Besides the spirit being the highest and most important aspect of man, the spirit is the deepest and most profound level of our being... The inner core of all non-organic mental-emotional problems is spiritual, not psychological. The cure is found in trusting and following the spiritual principles of the Bible, not the unproven theories and practices of psychotherapy.[8]

Literature in the field of Christian counseling has recognized the need to relate doctrine to counseling practice. In *Curing the Heart: A Model for Biblical Counseling*, the authors state,

> It has been our observation that much of what passes for biblical or Christian counseling flows from a study or awareness of popular ideas with Bible verses tacked on...The truly biblical counselor understands that he is a theologian...He will be conversant on essential doctrines such as regeneration, justification, sanctification, repentance and forgiveness. Theology—understanding God and His universe and His ways of working in man—will be a passion.[9]

The thesis of trichotomy as explored in Part 1 is integral to the biblical doctrine that is applied in counseling ministry.

A comprehensive textbook by the American Association of Christian Counselors (AACC) also notes the importance of the theological roots of counseling:

> The Christian counselor must be able to diagnose correctly the theological malady that is at the heart of humanity's dilemma...Unless we repent and turn, we will become destructive, abandon our postings, and vandalize the very

shalom of God...The diagnosis offered regarding humanity's potential and fallenness is accurate; the prescription for the treatment is a radical and God-provisioned one... The cumulative impact of what Jesus Christ does for the believing sinner results in the creation of a new person empowered to taste life in a new and healthful manner. That person is in union with Christ. Union with Christ is really the central issue in the message to be shared with clients... Grace is the at the core of all Christian ministry, especially counseling.[10]

The analysis quoted above confirms the purpose of this book, which is to clarify the nature of the believer's union with Christ through an explanation of the role of the human spirit.

Use of Trichotomy in the Field of Biblical Counseling

The Exchanged Life Model

A biblical understanding of the means of abundant living in Christ should be foundational to one's counseling approach. The "Exchanged life" is one of the titles of deeper life sanctification. The phrase evidently originated in the devotional writing of J. Hudson Taylor, founder of China Inland Mission. It is a scriptural concept, alluding to Isaiah 40:31:

> But those who wait on the LORD
> Shall renew their strength;
> They shall mount up with wings like eagles,
> They shall run and not be weary,
> They shall walk and not faint.

The word "renew" is a translation of the Hebrew *chalaph*, meaning "to change or exchange." *Hudson Taylor's Spiritual Secret* testifies how he came to personally appropriate the truth of Galatians 2:20: "I have been crucified with Christ; it is no longer I who live, but Christ lives in me; and the life which I now live in the flesh I live by faith in the Son of God, who loved me and gave Himself for me."[11]

The truth of the believer's union with Christ has been emphasized in the 20th century by groups such as the Keswick movement (e.g., Evan Hopkins, F.B. Meyer, Andrew Murray) and the Capernwray Bible Schools (founded by Major Ian Thomas). Recent examples of Exchanged Life teaching include books by Stephen Olford and Neil Anderson. Olford's book, *Not I But Christ*, has an introduction by Billy Graham and endorsements by other prominent pastors and teachers (which indicate that these truths are appreciated by many evangelicals). Anderson and Freedom in Christ Ministries have been popularized through his books such as *Victory Over the Darkness*. This message and their Discipleship Counseling approach focuses on God's resources for living.

The perspective of *Christ as life* should be treasured by all believers, since it is clearly described by our Lord in His metaphor of the vine and branches in John 15:1-8. It was central to Paul's testimony and teaching as well (Gal 2:20; Col 3:1-3). For instance, Romans 5:10 declares, "For if when we were enemies we were reconciled to God through the death of His Son, much more, having been reconciled, we shall be *saved by His life*." F. J. Huegel, in *Bone of His Bone*, gave a thorough presentation of deeper life sanctification. In the book's final chapter, Huegel insisted that if this view of sanctification were biblical, it should radically affect Christian ministry.[12] While he itemized the implications of identification with Christ on the ministries of church, prayer, and missions, it obvious that it should also directly impact biblical counseling.

Exchanged Life Counseling is based on the Keswick view of sanctification and usually employs a trichotomous model of man. The believer's co-crucifixion and co-resurrection with Christ is not only positional; it is also legal and spiritual. While agreeing with the importance of correcting sinful behavior (as in the Nouthetic model), this approach sees the root problem in the believer as his/her "flesh." The essential remedy is the applied Cross (full surrender, appropriating identification by faith, spiritual victory, and self-denying discipleship). The emphasis is on *being* in order to *do*.

For by grace you have been saved through faith, and that not of yourselves; it is the gift of God, not of works, lest anyone should boast. For we are His workmanship, created

in Christ Jesus for good works, which God prepared before-
hand that we should walk in them" (Eph 2:8-10).

Exchanged Life counselors have found that the tripartite na-
ture of man (as spirit, soul, and body) is crucial to communi-
cate clearly the precise truths of the believer's union with Christ.
Charles Solomon observed,

> Because most Christians see no practical relevance in hold-
> ing to strong conclusions about their immaterial makeup,
> the discussion of dichotomy and trichotomy is viewed as
> theological hairsplitting. But if Christians can be shown that
> a clear understanding of the soul's relationship to the spirit
> of man can clarify and solve practical problems that face
> him everyday, the distinction may be worth understand-
> ing...Because we have seen the strong interdependency of
> identity and acceptance in man, we need to examine both
> models of man [dichotomy versus trichotomy] to see which
> better accommodates an explanation of the cause and solu-
> tion to these needs and which of the two is more consistent
> with biblical language. Finding a spiritual model of man
> [trichotomy] will aid the believer in understanding his in-
> terpersonal functioning and his standing before God.[13]

A Christ-centered counseling approach must be anchored in and
be congruent with a model of man which encourages the apprehension and appropriation of one's identification with Christ.
Discerning a scriptural model of man will aid the believer in
understanding his fellowship with God, his inner functioning
and the spiritual resources necessary for abundant living.

Solomon has observed the importance of defending trichotomy in counseling. The need for this vindication was exemplified in a problem encountered with a Christian ministry
in Europe in 1983. He recalls,

> A medical doctor, Kurt Blatter, wanted to use our approach
> to counseling in a holistic setting where there would be
> treatment for spirit, soul, and body. (He went ahead and
> developed the center in Langenthal Switzerland.) Dr. Paul
> Kaschel and I went there to meet with him, and everything
> went well until we met with his theological committee which
> summarily rejected our model once they found that we be-

lieved that man has a spirit. They labeled me a heretic for having such a belief. Paul Kaschel went back to Europe and taught, but he needed to modify the Grace Fellowship model by superimposing a heart over both soul and spirit so he could teach the basic message.[14]

Alleviating the concerns of that theological committee could have opened the door to more networking with holistic Christian counseling.

The clarity that trichotomy brings to sanctification facilitates the communication and apprehension of deeper life truths, yet it is not always explicit in books with a Galatians 2:20 orientation. This is demonstrated in Elmer Towns' survey of deeper life devotional literature.[15] Although Exchanged Life counselors highly value the practical use body, soul and spirit diagrams, this does not exempt them from benefiting from devotional literature that does not make a trichotomist model of man explicit.[16]

Ministries Using Trichotomy in Biblical Counseling

As noted in the chapter five, for most of the 1900's there was a gap between the deeper life sanctification message and the models of Christian counseling as employed by Christian psychiatrists, psychotherapists, and pastoral counselors. Charles Solomon made a valuable contribution by bringing the Exchanged Life message into a practical, short-term counseling process. In the early sixties, Solomon was an engineer with Martin Marietta who was living a "defeated life." He repeatedly turned to God for help. After months of study in God's Word, the solution of Christ as life (Col 3:4) was revealed to him. Eager to share this message with others, Solomon resigned his position and began a Christ-centered counseling ministry in his home. Through personal counseling and seminars, Christians recovered from chronic problems through appropriating their identification with Christ. *Handbook to Happiness* explains the essential content of this model, also known as "Spirituotherapy." Diagrams used in this text clearly distinguish spirit, soul, and body and the functions of each. In May 1969, he founded Grace Fellowship International (GFI). This organization, now based in Pigeon Forge, Tennessee, has helped launch many similar ministries in North America and has affiliated centers in several other countries.

Another prominent Exchanged Life counseling ministry is Lifetime Guarantee Ministries, based in Fort Worth, Texas. It was founded by Bill Gillham, a former professor of psychology at Oklahoma State University. His book, *Lifetime Guarantee*, presents a definitive explanation of the Exchanged Life concepts. Included are diagrams identifying the spirit, soul, body and their respective functions. Bill, Anabel, and their son Preston Gillham, have been actively teaching this message through counseling, radio, and conferences.[17]

Some Exchanged Life Counseling centers joined together to form an alliance known as the Association of Exchanged Life Ministries (AELM). There are currently over fifty member ministries and affiliated individuals. A.E.L.M. has published *Foundations of Exchanged Life Counseling*. In this text, Richard Hall gives a concise overview of the essential principles of this counseling model.[18] Hall clearly identifies man as spirit, soul, and body (portrayed in 16 diagrams). These diagrams include the symbolism of the tabernacle as illustrative of trichotomy. They clarify the difference between the unregenerate person, the carnal believer, and the spiritual believer. Similar diagrams are featured in the conference manuals of Grace Fellowship International and A.E.L.M.

Bob Hoekstra of Living in Christ Ministries (Costa Mesa, CA) has written *How to Counsel God's Way*. He presents seminars on this subject and gives a thorough, biblical basis for the whole counseling process. He protests the trend of integrating secular psychology in Christian counseling. His teaching emphasizes the abundant life truths of sanctification in Christ. Hoekstra summarized the problem and its cure, using a trichotomous model of man. Notice his confirmation of the survey of redemptive history in chapter 4:

> God created people to be alive in their spirits, able to relate and respond to Him, as Adam and Eve did before their sinful rebellion. This spiritual life was to be expressed through the soul of man, through his mind and emotions and will, through his personality. This immaterial reality of human experience was to reside in a physical body that did what it was told to do. However, man rebelled, and his spirit died. Since then, these human bodies, wherein sin dwells

[Rom 6:6b], have been exerting a controlling influence upon Adam's race. Man's profound need is to have this body of sin removed from its dominating position, having it "done away with," or "rendered powerless." To provide for this need, God supplies a remedy, one that man and his speculative theories could never produce. God's drastic solution is the spiritual execution of the original tenant, the person who first lived in what became our body of sin...Through faith in Christ, through identification with Him in His death and resurrection, the old man can be replaced by a new creature in Christ [2 Cor 5:17]... This new, spiritually alive person can increasingly say no to this body of sin...Through our identification with the Lord Jesus, we have been resurrected with Him into an entirely new spiritual life. This is the hope that the people of God have and need to hear.[19]

Hoekstra's counseling approach diagnoses man's spiritual problem and applies God's provision through our union with Christ. This model is clarified through a trichotomous model of man.

A program that has been used to train laypersons for Christian counseling is *How Can I Help?* by W. H. Hunt. The course is designed primarily to equip helpers to handle telephone counseling situations. Other applications include support groups, recovery groups, and visitation ministry. Hunt's course uses a model of man as spirit, soul, and body.[20]

The Therapon Institute of Crockett, Texas claims to be the largest, most credentialed faith based counseling school in that state. Founded by Dr. Paul Carlin and Jeri Carlin, this residential school and distance education program originated through their ministry in the criminal justice system. The school's credentialing policy was authorized by the government's call for faith-based institutions to develop alternative licensing procedures that would not compromise their values and spiritual mission. Therapon offers paraprofessional credentials of Pastoral Counselor, Licensed Belief Therapist, and Certified Reentry Crisis Counselor. One of the six core courses in their curriculum is based on *Handbook for Christ-Centered Counseling*, by Charles Solomon. As presented in that volume, this counseling ministry uses an explicit trichotomous model of man.

The Center for Biblical Counseling in Sunnyvale, California has a vision to equip local churches with Christ-centered, grace-oriented counseling ministry. The director, Greg Burts, has developed counseling materials to use in personal ministry and counselor training. In his book, *Strategic Biblical Counseling*, he presents a model for pastors and lay counselors that uses spirit, soul, and body diagrams and a sanctification based process for resolving problems. His wife, Altha, has written a helpful autobiography and additional course material using trichotomy.[21]

Healing prayer is a specialized aspect of counseling. Ed Smith leads Theophostic Ministries (Campbellsville, Kentucky) and has developed an helping approach known as Theophostic Prayer Ministry. This methodology and training has expanded to form an international association of pastors, counselors and lay helpers. In his training videos and manual, Smith refers to a spirit, soul, and body model of man. Many evangelicals have cautiously started to incorporate some degree of healing prayer into their counseling and pastoral care ministries.[22]

Hope for the Heart is the biblical counseling organization in Dallas, Texas led by author and teacher June Hunt. She has published one hundred Counseling Keys that cover the common problems faced by people today. Hunt integrates the truth of the believer's identification with Christ into her resources. In the Counseling Key on the Holy Spirit, the three aspects of a person are identified and defined.[23] She credits Ian Thomas' *The Saving Life of Christ*, as the most influential book in her life (apart from the Bible). Thomas explicitly refers to man as spirit, soul, and body in chapter 3 of that book and elucidates it in a subsequent book *The Mystery of Godliness*. Hope for the Heart also conducts five day Biblical Counseling Institutes. They produce daily teaching and call-in radio programs that address common problems from a biblical perspective.

The Institute in Basic Life Principles (IBLP) in Oak Brook, Illinois is best known for their basic seminar, authored and presented by Bill Gothard. Over 2.5 million people have attended this seminar, which is aimed at helping people resolve their problems by applying biblical principles of life. I.B.L.P. has various educational programs and training facilities. The seminars and their course on *Effective Biblical Counseling* employ the spirit, soul, and body perspective on man's makeup.[24]

In Touch, with Dr. Charles Stanley, is a popular and far-reaching radio and TV broadcast ministry. Their telephone counselors give personalized counsel to listeners and send relevant literature, including Solomon's *Handbook to Happiness* and *Ins & Out of Rejection*. The programs originate from First Baptist Church, Atlanta, Georgia. That church has developed a biblical counseling ministry currently led by Dr. Al Scardino. The staff and lay counselors employ an Exchanged Life model that describes man as spirit, soul, and body.

The first edition of this book was done as a project for the doctoral program of Luther Rice Seminary in Lithonia, Georgia. For over a decade this institution has featured Discipleship Counseling as an area of specialization. Courses in Discipleship counseling and spiritual formation have included material including the trichotomous makeup of man.

Summary

Although this survey of ministries and authors is not exhaustive, it indicates that the biblical doctrine of trichotomy has a significant role in current biblical counseling ministries. If a counselor using this model of man is criticized on the basis of biblical psychology, the material presented in this book could equip him to respond on biblical, theological, and historical grounds. The rise of scholarly treatments of trichotomy in the 19th and 20th centuries facilitated a more precise study of progressive sanctification. This development gave impetus to deeper life teaching and its subsequent counseling model. Psychology continues to explore man's "soul" through observable actions, thoughts, responses, and relationships. To interpret this data and remain faithful to God's Word, the Christian counselor needs an accurate understanding of man's constitutional makeup, personal needs, and the gracious remedy found in Christ.

¹ John MacArthur, *The Sufficiency of Christ* (Dallas: Word Publishing, 1991), 69,70.

² Gerald Corey, *Theory and Practice of Counseling and Psychotherapy* (Monterey, CA: Brooks/Cole Publishing Co., 1977), 185.

³ Jay E. Adams, *The Christian Counselor's Manual* (Grand Rapids: Baker Book House, 1973), 93. Cf. John C. Brogan, *Self Confrontation: A Manual for In–Depth Biblical Discipleship* (Palm Dessert, CA: Biblical Counseling Foundation, 1991).

⁴ Lawrence O. Richards and Gib Martin, *A Theology of Personal Ministry: Spiritual Giftedness in the Local Church* (Grand Rapids: Zondervan, 1981), 11.

⁵ O. Quentin Hyder, *The Christian's Handbook of Psychiatry* (Old Tappan, NJ: Fleming H. Revell,1971), 51.

⁶ Jeffery Boyd, "One's Self Concept and Biblical Theology," *Journal of the Evangelical Theological Society*, 40 (1997): 223. Cf. Frank Minirth, *Christian Psychiatry*.

⁷ Lenski, *Interpretation of First Thessalonians*, 367 [Emphasis added]. (The first part of this quote was included in chapter 4.)

⁸ Martin and Deidre Bobgan, *The Psychological Way and the Spiritual Way* (Minneapolis, MN: Bethany Fellowship, 1979), 143, 145.

⁹ Howard Eyrich and William Hines, *Curing the Heart* (Mentor: 2002), 57. This Nouthetic model of biblical counseling is based on the Reformed view of sanctification and usually a dichotomous model of man. However, the president of the International Association of Biblical Counselors has written a critique of secular psychology that maintains a trichotomous view of man (Ed Bulkley, *Why Christians Can't Trust Psychology*, 339). This admonition-oriented model has reminded ministers that they are "competent to counsel" through a Spirit-filled life and a skillful use of God's Word. We also commend them for being consistent in applying their theology to counseling practice. If dichotomy is maintained, however, then the believer's co-crucifixion with Christ is interpreted as only positional; it does not affect the spirit of the believer. The movement toward the *heart* of man in Nouthetic Counseling confirms the importance of biblical psychology.

[10] Ron Hawkins, Edward Hindson, and Tim Clinton, "Theological Roots," in *Competent Christian Counseling*, eds., Timothy Clinton and George Ohlschlanger (Colorado Springs: Waterbrook Press, 2002), 1:108, 110.

[11] Howard and Geraldine Taylor, *Hudson Taylor's Spiritual Secret* (Chicago: Moody Press, 1932), 157.

[12] F. J. Huegel, *Bone of His Bone* (Grand Rapids: Zondervan, 1972), 93-101. Cf. W. Ian Thomas, *The Saving Life of Christ* (Grand Rapids: Zondervan, 1965).

[13] Charles R. Solomon, *Handbook to Acceptance* (Wheaton, IL: Tyndale House, 1982), 99-100. Cf. *Handbook to Happiness* (Tyndale, 1971) and *Handbook for Christ–Centered Counseling* (Sevierville, TN: Solomon Publications, 1977). Solomon completed the Doctor of Education degree in Spirituotherapy at University of Northern Colorado through which he pioneered a model for counseling people from an "Exchanged Life" perspective.

[14] Charles Solomon and Stoney Shaw, *The Solomon Institute in Spirituotherapy* (Sevierville, TN: Grace Fellowship, 1998), 4. Similar objections are still forthcoming. In a recent journal article criticizing the Exchanged Life and trichotomy, the authors appeal to issues addressed in chapter 7 above. Cf. chapter 1, footnote 4.

[15] Elmer Towns, *Understanding the Deeper Life* (Old Tappan, NJ: Revell, 1988). www.elmertowns.com.

[16] See V. Raymond Edman, *They Found the Secret* (Grand Rapids: Zondervan Publishing House, 1960); Stephen Olford, *Not I, But Christ* (Wheaton, IL: Crossway Books, 1995); Miles Stanford, *The Complete Green Letters* (Grand Rapids: Zondervan, 1975).

[17] Bill Gillham, *Lifetime Guarantee* (Eugene, OR: Harvest House, 1993), 27, 71-74.

[18] Richard Hall, *Foundations of Exchanged Life Counseling* (Aurora Co: Cross-Life Expressions, 1993), 15-18, 44-51.

[19] Bob Hoekstra, *Counseling God's Way* (Costa Mesa, CA: Living in Christ Ministries, 1999), 207-209 [Emphasis added].

[20] W. H. Hunt, *How Can I Help?* (Tampa, FL: Christian Helplines, 2000), 150, 176-85.

[21] H. Greg Burts, *Strategic Biblical Counseling* (Enumclaw, WA: Pleasant Word, 2002), 48-50. Cf. Altha Burts, *Come Up Higher* (Enumclaw, WA: Pleasant Word, 2005).

[22] Ed Smith, *Beyond Tolerable Recovery* (Alathia Publishing, 1999), 398. The Christian Research Institute has been in dialogue with Smith, who has clarified some of his material and policies. CRI has published an evaluation on TPM and considers it within the scope of orthodoxy (www.Equip.org).

[23] June Hunt, *Counseling Key: The Holy Spirit* (Dallas, TX: Hope for the Heart), 6, and January 2007 newsletter.

[24] *A Comprehensive Course in Effective Counseling* (Oak Brook, IL: Institute in Basic Life Principles, n.d.), 1:9-14.

Dennis and Rita Bennett wrote a step-by-step guide for resolving problems biblically using an explicit spirit, soul, and body model—*Trinity of Man: The Three Dimensions of Healing and Wholeness* (Plainfield, NJ: Logos, 1979).

Conclusion

This study of biblical psychology has surveyed various models of man en route to advocating the case for humans as spirit, soul, and body persons who have been created in God's image. The biblical word studies and a sketch of redemption history have substantiated the basis for trichotomy and demonstrated its relevance in interpreting pivotal events and relevant doctrines.

The model of holistic trichotomy may facilitate further research and dialogue toward a consensus concerning the unity of man's person, the obvious duality in his material and immaterial elements, and the ontological distinction between soul and spirit.

The biblical counseling association to which I belong helps struggling Christians regain spiritual, psychological,— and sometimes physical—health. Decades of clinical experience have demonstrated the practical value of a clarified model of man in recognizing and appropriating the believer's identification with Christ in His death, burial, resurrection, and ascension.

At a popular level, trichotomy has won wide appeal through deeper life literature and evangelical preaching. As students are reminded of trichotomy's acceptance in the early church, the reason for its disfavor in the west following the fourth century controversy, and its reaffirmation by Luther, this model of man may be examined more objectively on its own merits. German and English theologians of recent centuries have presented scholarly volumes in support of a more literal view of the references to the spirit/soul/body distinctions that were especially clarified in the epistles of Paul.

The research presented in this book is offered as a ministry to the body of Christ with the prayer for greater accuracy in discerning the makeup of man's constitutional elements, the soul/spirit distinction, and the faculties related to each. May a renewed interest in biblical psychology support the vital role of Christian discipleship and counseling in these stress-filled times.

MAN AS SPIRIT, SOUL AND BODY:

APPENDICES

A STUDY OF BIBLICAL PSYCHOLOGY

Appendix A
Transliterated Biblical Vocabulary

The following is a list of Old and New Testament terms referred to in this book with their dictionary forms.

Hebrew

adamah	אדמה	ground
basar	בשר	body, flesh
chalaph	חלף	change, renew
leb	לב	heart
hayim	חיים	life (plural)
moth tamuth	מות תמות	shall surely die
nephesh	נפש	soul
neshama	נשמה	breath
ruach	רוח	spirit
sheol	שאול	grave, hell
Yom Kippur	יום הכפרים	Day of Atonement

Greek

anagennao	αναγενναω	give new birth
apokueo	αποκυεω	to give birth
bios	βιος	life
boulomai	βουλομαι	will
duo	δυο	two
en	εν	in
ek	εκ	out
gennao	γενναω	be a father, beget
hagios	αγιος	holy
kardia	καρδια	heart
logos	λογος	word
nous	νους	mind

oloklaros	ολοκλερος	whole, entire
paliggenesia	παλιγγενεσια	regeneration
phroneo	φρονεο	think, regard
pneuma	πνευμα	spirit
pneumatikos	πνευματικος	spiritual
psuche	ψυχε	soul
psuchikos	ψυχικος	natural, soulical
sarkikos	σαρκικος	carnal, fleshly
sarx	σαρξ	flesh
soma	σομα	body
somatikos	σοματικος	bodily, physical
suneidesis	συνειδεσις	conscience
temno	τεμνω	to cut
thumos	θυμος	anger, breath
thelo	θελω	will
tricha	τριχα, τρεις	three
zoe	ζωη	life

Appendix B
Diagrams Used to Illustrate Trichotomy

The Unsaved Person

WHAT IS WRONG WITH ME?

Man is dead in relation to God.
*"You... were dead in
trespasses and sins"*
Ephesians 2:1

Man has a darkened mind and
damaged emotions;
he is self-centered.
*"For the natural man does not
understand the things of God,
for they are spiritually
appraised"*
1 Corinthians 2:14

Man cannot do the "work" that
God created Him to do because
he lives in a sinful environment.
*"By the sweat of your brow
you will eat your food until you
return to the ground"*
Genesis 3:18

H. Greg Burts *Strategic Biblical Counseling,* 78.

A Sequence of Redemption and Sanctification

DIAGRAM 1
ADAM PRIOR TO THE FALL

RELATES TO OTHERS — **SOUL** | **SPIRIT** → RELATES TO GOD

PERSONALITY

INNOCENT SPIRIT

BODY

RELATES TO ENVIRONMENT

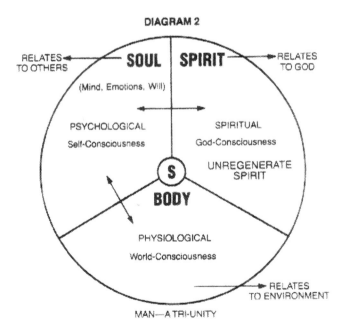

DIAGRAM 2

RELATES TO OTHERS — **SOUL** | **SPIRIT** → RELATES TO GOD

(Mind, Emotions, Will)

PSYCHOLOGICAL
Self-Consciousness

SPIRITUAL
God-Consciousness

S

UNREGENERATE SPIRIT

BODY

PHYSIOLOGICAL
World-Consciousness

RELATES TO ENVIRONMENT

MAN—A TRI-UNITY

DIAGRAM 5

SOUL | **SPIRIT**

1. INFERIORITY
2. INSECURITY
3. INADEQUACY
4. GUILT ⟨ REAL (sin) / IMAGINARY
5. WORRY, DOUBTS, FEARS

FAMILY, WORK, ETC

1. SALVATION
2. ASSURANCE
3. SECURITY
4. ACCEPTANCE
5. TOTAL COMMITMENT, SURRENDER (Rom. 12:1)

FRUSTRATION

HOSTILITY

MIND
1. FANTASY
2. SCHIZOPHRENIA
3. PARANOIA
4. OBSESSIVE THOUGHTS

EMOTIONS
1. DEPRESSION
2. ANXIETY

S

C

BODY

Tension headache or migraine, nervous stomach leading to peptic ulcer, hives, skin rashes, allergies, asthma, some arthritis, spastic colon, palpitations of heart, respiratory ailments, compulsive eating, fatigue, insomnia, escape in sleep, hypertension, etc.

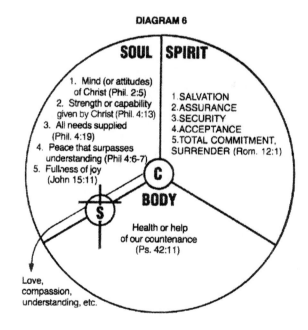

DIAGRAM 6

SOUL | **SPIRIT**

1. Mind (or attitudes) of Christ (Phil. 2:5)
2. Strength or capability given by Christ (Phil. 4:13)
3. All needs supplied (Phil. 4:19)
4. Peace that surpasses understanding (Phil 4:6-7)
5. Fullness of joy (John 15:11)

1. SALVATION
2. ASSURANCE
3. SECURITY
4. ACCEPTANCE
5. TOTAL COMMITMENT, SURRENDER (Rom. 12:1)

C

S

BODY

Health or help of our countenance (Ps. 42:11)

Love, compassion, understanding, etc.

Charles Solomon, *Handbook to Happiness*, 15-35.

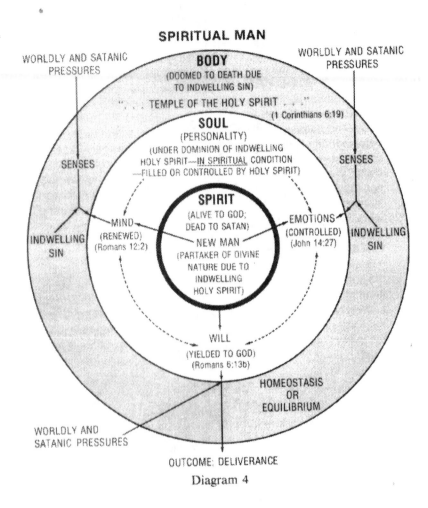

Diagram 4

Charles Solomon, *Handbook for Christ-Centered Counseling*, 35.

Man as Spirit, Soul, and Body

Appendix C
Physical, Soulical, and Spiritual Orientations in Counseling

A comic strip from the Peanuts series by Charles Schulz features Lucy in her make-shift stand with its posted sign: "Psychiatric help 5 cents. The doctor is IN." Charlie Brown has once again visited Lucy's booth for some counseling:

Lucy: "I've been thinking about your case a lot lately."

Charlie Brown: "That's gratifying."

Lucy: "You know what your trouble is, Charlie Brown? You don't have a personal philosophy. You need to develop a philosophy that will carry you through times of stress. Can you do that? Can you develop a personal philosophy? Think, Charlie Brown, think!"

Charlie Brown: (Contemplating) "Life is like an ice cream cone. You have to learn to lick it."

Lucy: (Running away hysterically) "That's the most stupid philosophy I've ever heard! I can't do anything for someone who has a philosophy like that! You're hopeless, Charlie Brown!"

Charlie Brown: "It's hard to develop a real personal philosophy in less than twenty minutes."[1]

Apparently, Lucy was never trained to handle the troubles of good old Charlie Brown! She did have a point, though: we need a personal belief system that will carry us through times of stress. But when our understanding of ourselves, life, and the Lord still leaves us with chronic mental, emotional, and relational problems, we can look for some counseling help.

One of the challenges in deciding to get help, however, is to sort out what kind of counseling approach to use. One way to put counseling options in context is to identify three broad categories of formal treatment of mental and emotional disorders.

First, the *psychiatrist* is trained as a medical doctor that is oriented to treat clients through medication. This doctor specializes in organically based problems and uses drugs such as antipsychotics (as in treating schizophrenia), lithium (as in treating bipolar disorders/manic-depressive cycles), antidepressants (for treating endogenous depression), and antianxiety drugs (for treating extreme anxiety).[2]

Secondly, the *psychologist* is trained as a therapist to diagnose and treat problems of the "soul" (Gk. psuche). Secular models of psychological counseling include: Psychoanalytic Therapy, Existential-Humanistic Therapy, Client-Centered Therapy, Gestalt Therapy, Transactional Analysis, Behavior Therapy, Rational-Emotive Therapy, and Reality Therapy. There are also versions of such secular models in which therapists, who identify themselves as Christians, seek to counsel in a way that is compatible with their faith.

Thirdly, the *pastoral counselor* should be trained to diagnose and facilitate recovery from spiritual problems that also affect the soul, and usually the body as well. Pastoral counseling extends beyond "clergy", including the ministry of any equipped believer who provides biblical counsel. This assistance ranges from vocational biblical counselors to others who are ministering on an informal basis.

Paul identified three aspects of our makeup that correspond to the three categories of counseling just noted: "Now may the God of peace Himself sanctify you completely; and may your whole *spirit, soul, and body* be preserved blameless at the coming of our Lord Jesus Christ. He who calls you is faithful, who also will do it" (1 Thes 5:23-24).

What are the distinctive features of these parts of the human being? The human *spirit* is the immaterial aspect of a person that includes the faculties of conscience, intuition, and communion. The *soul* is the immaterial part of us that includes the faculties of mind, will, emotions, and affections. The *body*, of course, is the material aspect of our makeup, which includes our organ systems, senses, appetites etc. These parts of the human being also have distinctive roles in our relationships.

We primarily relate to *God* via the human spirit (Rom 8:16, John 4:23,24); we primarily relate to other *people* via the soul, and we primarily relate to the *material world* through the body. Although we are one in personhood, these aspects of our makeup need to be accurately discerned.[3]

Although much pastoral counseling is eclectic and psychology-oriented, the biblical role of pastor/discipler leads to a model of counseling that is Christ-centered and grace-oriented. Such ministry should function as remedial discipleship under the guidance of the Holy Spirit—the ultimate Therapist.[4]

In his book, *Called to Counsel,* John Cheydleur identifies the value of interpersonal counseling and then notes pastoral counseling's relationship to the spiritual life:

> Pastoral counseling often includes the concerns of other counseling disciplines, but the purpose is holy and requires a more complete sensitivity than the other three approaches psychiatry, psychotherapy, and clinical social work. The focus of spiritual counseling is nothing less than the reconciliation of the three dimensions of life with the powerful and critical fourth dimension of the spirit.[5]

One's view of redemption and sanctification is foundational to clarifying one's counseling strategy. Note this observation by a secular writer on the centrality of one's belief system in determining the right counseling model:

> It is my conviction that our views of human nature and the basic assumptions that undergird our views of the therapeutic process have significant implications for the way we develop our therapeutic practices...a central task is to make our assumptions explicit and conscious, so that we can establish some consistency between our beliefs about human nature and the way we implement our procedures in counseling or therapy.[6]

A. B. Simpson's book, *Christ in You: The Christ-Life and the Self-Life* deals directly with the issues of deeper life sanctification. Commenting on Christ's high priestly prayer in John 17, Simpson observed, "This was the last prayer that Christ offered for His people: 'That I myself may be in them' (v. 26b)...Oh, if we want this prayer fulfilled, we must enter into the meaning of this message and never stop short of its actual experience."[7] Drawing on the heritage of deeper-life writers, Dr. Charles Solomon developed a model of counseling that focuses on sharing this message and helping believers appropriate their union with Christ experientially. He formulated a strategic, short-term model of biblical counseling following his own spiritual breakthrough.[8] This process helps the counselee understand:

1. The root cause of problems such as inferiority, inadequacy, insecurity, worry, doubts, and fears
2. Basic spiritual needs that only God can meet
3. The formative influences of being overtly or covertly rejected by others
4. The root causes of emotional tension (depression, anxiety), and mental dysfunction (fantasy, paranoia, obsessive thoughts etc.)
5. The role of personal identity
6. The biblical teaching of the believer's union with Christ in His death, burial, resurrection, and ascension
7. The necessity of applying the work of the Cross in exchanging the "self-life" for the "Christ-life".[9]

Although psychiatry can assist individuals with genuine, organically-based problems, and temporary medical support to help address root issues, the Christ-centered counselor does not merely seek to merely alleviate the counselee's symptoms, or help them strengthen their coping mechanisms. In fact, often the believer's desperation best prepares them to give up on themselves and trust Christ absolutely as their source of living! (Rom. 7:15-8:11).

It is fascinating to see how people's lives begin to change for the better when Galatians 2:20 is appropriated: "I have been crucified with Christ; it is no longer I who live, but Christ lives in me; and the life which I now live in the flesh I live by faith in the Son of God, who loved me and gave Himself for me." Turmoil in the soul is replaced by peace, joy, and contentment to the extent that the believer is focused on Christ as Savior, Lord, and Life (2 Cor. 12:9). This approach is simply profound and profoundly simple.

Man As Spirit, Soul, and Body

People can also expect to recover from stress related health problems when the Christ-life resolves the root causes—namely, the self-life. Such psychologically-induced conditions may include tension headache, nervous stomach, ulcers, hives, skin rashes, allergies, asthma, spastic colon, heart palpitations, breathing ailments, fatigue, insomnia etc.

While writing this article I received a phone call from a counselee who had a dramatic deeper life experience. He had a history of chronic tension headaches and was always popping Tylenols. However, in the year since he appropriated his identification with Christ he has had no more headaches! Then he counseled a brother who was hospitalized with symptoms of Crohn's disease who rapidly improved—to the amazement of the doctors.

Spirituotherapy credits the Holy Spirit Who uses the Word of God to progressively sanctify the believer, illumining the fuller implications of the disciple's union with Christ. God's Spirit can give care and cure; He indwells every true believer (John 16:12-15). Truly the Doctor is IN.

Presenting counseling seminars internationally, I often hear believers testify of the radical benefits they experience as the truths of their identification with Christ begins to sink in. One sister who attended an event in Romania was depressed to the extent of suicidal thoughts. The following day—after being led to the foot of the Cross to appropriate her spiritual identity in Christ—she was radiant with His joy and Life!

All glory for restoring the soul goes to the Spirit of God. Cheydleur testified,

> "The better we become at spiritual counseling, the less pride we will take in it. Every time God uses us to release joy in a previously troubled person, we will realize that the power that has healed the person is of God and does not stem from our righteousness or ability. It is most effective when we empty ourselves and allow God to bring healing and wholeness through us."[10]

In counseling, consider the how the physical, psychological, and spiritual parts of a person are involved. Seek the Lord's wisdom and His abundant provision in Christ. The Doctor is IN! There is hope because of our Wonderful Counselor (Isa. 9:6).

[1] Charles M. Schulz, *Peanuts Classics* (Holt, Rinehart & Winston; N.Y.)

[2] R. J. Salinger, 'Psychopharmacology' in *Baker Encyclopedia of Psychology*, ed. David Benner (Grand Rapids: Baker), 944-949.

[3] John Woodward, *Man as Spirit, Soul, and Body: A Study of Biblical Psychology* (Pigeon Forge, TN: Grace Fellowship International, 2007).

[4] Charles Solomon, *Handbook for Christ-Centered Counseling* (Sevierville, TN: Solomon Publications, 1977).

[5] John Cheydleur, *Called to Counsel* (Tyndale House, 1999), 38.

[6] Gerald Corey, *Theory and Practice of Counseling and Psychotherapy* (Monterey, CA: Brooks/Cole Publishing Co., 1977),185.

[7] A. B. Simpson, *Christ in You: The Christ-Life and the Self-Life* (Camp Hill, PA: Christian Publications, 1997), p.33.

[8] Gerlad E. McGraw, *Launch Out: A Theology of Dynamic Sanctification* (Camp Hill, PA: Christian Publications) 253-54.

[9] Charles Solomon, *Handbook to Happiness* (Tyndale House). cf. *Handbook for Christ Centered Counseling*.

[10] Cheydleur, 59.

Appendix D
The Relevance of the Trichotomy of Man in Spiritual Warfare

Frances Manuel wrote an insightful book on confronting demonic oppression. In *Though an Host Should Encamp*, she recounted what she had learned from Scripture and personal experience in spiritual warfare. Manuel found that the soul/spirit distinction was relevant in determining how a Christian could be sealed with the Holy Spirit, yet obviously be under demonic oppression (Eph 6:10-18). The apostle Peter admonished,

> Be sober, be vigilant; because your adversary the devil walks about like a roaring lion, seeking whom he may devour. Resist him, steadfast in the faith, knowing that the same sufferings are experienced by your brotherhood in the world (1 Pet 5:8,9).

Manuel observed that, "...the spirit of the born-again believer, occupied by the Holy Spirit, cannot be also host to a demon, though body and soul may be."[1] She quoted the former chancellor of Wheaton College on this topic:

> I have recently read a comment written by the late Dr. V. Raymond Edman during the time of his editorship of *The Alliance Witness*, which I quote at this point, giving both question and answer:
>
> Q.   A dear Christian woman in our congregation is mentally ill. In her emotional disturbance she often speaks of committing suicide. Some of us believe we see indications of demon possession, but our pastor contends that no born-again Christian can be demon possessed, but rather is demon oppressed. What is your opinion?

A.   This sad situation may be entirely a physical matter and there should be prayer with faith for full healing and restoration. On the other hand it might be a case of demon possession. Textbooks on Christian doctrine all teach, as far as I know, that a truly born-again Christian cannot be demonized. This is not stated in the Bible but is inferred from the fact that a believer is born again of the Holy Spirit, and that the Holy Spirit and a demon cannot occupy the same place. The latter statement is true: a demon cannot enter the regenerated spirit of the Christian. *However, we are a tripartite being: spirit, soul, and body.* The unguarded Christian may have demon possession in the *soul* which would affect mental processes and emotions, or in the *body*, as was the case of the woman who had "a spirit of infirmity eighteen years, and was bowed together, and could in no wise lift up herself" (Luke 13:11). Of her the Saviour said when He healed her, "Ought not this woman, being a daughter of Abraham, whom Satan hath bound, lo, these eighteen years, be loosed from this bond on the Sabbath day?" To say that a Christian cannot be demonized in any area of his life is a happy but inaccurate generalization.[2]

While agreeing with Edman's view, it seems preferable to avoid the terminology of *demon possession.* It would be less controversial to speak of the possibility of *demonic oppression.* These clarifications should help allay the fears of those who assume that intentional spiritual warfare is unscriptural or irrelevant for today. The wealth and walk of the Christian prepares him/her for spiritual warfare. As Paul admonished,

Finally, my brethren, be strong in the Lord and in the power of His might. Put on the whole armor of God, that you may be able to stand against the wiles of the devil. For we do not wrestle against flesh and blood, but against principalities, against powers, against the rulers of the darkness of this age, against spiritual hosts of wickedness in the heavenly places. Therefore take up the whole armor of God, that you may be able to withstand in the evil day, and having done all, to stand. Stand therefore, having girded your waist with truth, having put on the breastplate of righteousness, and having shod your feet with the preparation of the gospel of peace; above all, taking the shield of faith with which you will be able to quench all the fiery darts of the wicked one. And take the helmet of salvation, and the sword of the Spirit, which is the word of God; praying always with all prayer and supplication in the Spirit, being watchful to this end with all perseverance and supplication for all the saints (Eph 6:10-18).

The believer's spirit is sealed by the Holy Spirit Who gives us power over the forces of darkness: "You are of God, little children, and have overcome them, because He who is in you is greater than he who is in the world" (1 John 4:4). Yet, interfering thoughts, ideas, and temptations from the enemy are real dangers: "Therefore submit to God. Resist the devil and he will flee from you" (James 4:7).

¹ Frances Manuel, *Though an Host Should Encamp* (Sevierville, TN: Stout Hearted Publications/GFI) 46.

² "Questions Answered by the Editor," *The Alliance Witness,* 102 (April 26, 1967): 22, [emphasis added].

Ministries that relate freedom in Christ to counseling include the International Center for Biblical Counseling (Westfield, IN), Biblical Counseling Concepts (Colorado Springs, CO), and Freedom in Christ Ministries (Knoxville, TN).

Appendix E
The Believer's New Heart

M. R. De Haan, medical doctor and Bible teacher, told of a conversation he had with a neighbor in which he really got to the heart of things.

> It was the first time I met my neighbor, who had just moved in a few days before. He told me he had heart trouble and had sold his business on the advice of his doctor. He seemed quite surprised when I said, 'Yes, I know, and I understand you were born with a bad heart.' Emphatically he replied, 'Oh no, I had a heart attack just a year ago! Before that my heart was perfect.' 'But,' I added, 'I read just this morning that you were born with heart disease.' I referred him to what God says about the sinful human heart and the need of a new heart. It was the first time he had heard the real diagnosis of his heart condition. My good neighbor had physical heart trouble, but his spiritual heart condition was a much more serious problem.[1]

De Haan had an accurate prescription:

> There is only one remedy. A 'new heart' must be supplied by the Great Physician, Jesus. He does His work in us as we acknowledge our heart trouble and let Him operate by His grace and give us eternal life.[2]

This leads us to the question, What is the nature of the believer's new heart? This aspect of our life must be important; it is referred to over 750 times in the Scripture. For example, Proverbs advises, "Keep your heart with all diligence, For out of it spring the issues of life" (Prov. 4:23). The heart's importance is also indicated in the greatest commandment: "You shall love the LORD your God with all your heart, with all your soul, and with all your mind" (Matt. 22:37).

In his book, *Religious Affections*, Jonathan Edwards made a strong case for the central role of the heart in Christian life and worship. Edwards observed:

> That religion which God requires, and will accept, does not consist in weak, dull, and lifeless wishes, raising us but a little above a state of indifference. God, in His Word, greatly insists upon it, that we be good in earnest, 'fervent in spirit,' and our hearts vigorously engaged in religion: Romans 12:11, 'Be ye fervent in spirit, serving the Lord.' Deuteronomy 10:12, 'And now, Israel, what doth the Lord thy God require of thee, but to fear the Lord the God, to walk in all his ways, and to love him, and to serve the Lord thy God with all thy heart, and with all thy soul?' and chapter 6:4, 6, 'Hear, O Israel, the Lord our God is one Lord: And thou shalt love the Lord thy God with all thy heart, and with all thy might.' It is such a fervent vigorous engagedness of the heart in religion, that is the fruit of a real circumcision of the heart, or true regeneration, and that has the promises of life; Deut 30:6, 'And the Lord thy God will circumcise thine heart, and the heart of thy seed, to love the Lord thy God with all thy heart, and with all thy soul, that thou mayest live. (KJV)'[2]

A study of biblical passages mentioning the "heart" indicates that it corresponds to person's innermost being—especially as it relates to affections and love. The heart reflects what is valued and treasured in life. Hebrews 4:12 indicates that the inner, unseen you is comprised of soul and spirit: "For the word of God is living and powerful, and sharper than any two-edged sword, piercing even to the division of soul and spirit...God's truth reaches our innermost being; it is a discerner of the thoughts and intents of the heart." Is heart identical with either soul or spirit? Not exactly; nor is the heart an additional part of us. Rather, *the heart is a cluster of faculties that is the seat of reflection, motivation, and affection involving both soul and spirit.*

References to the believer's heart convey mixed messages; some refer to sinful tendencies, other passages describe the new, righteous heart. How do we reconcile these differences? Just as the physical organ of the heart has chambers, consider two chambers of the believer's heart: the "soul chamber" and the "spirit chamber."

The Soul Chamber of the Heart

The "soul chamber of the heart" is subject to the influence of the flesh, the world, and the devil. References of warning are addressed to the soul/heart. When referring to the flesh tendencies in the soul chamber, the prophet declared, "The heart is deceitful above all things, And desperately wicked; Who can know it?" (Jer 17:9). This would apply to the spirit of an unsaved person. Similarly, the apostle Paul confessed that in our flesh "dwells nothing good" (Rom 7:18; cf. Matt 15:19).

Other passages about the heart are directed at the soul's choice to love and value either what is evil (Deut 11:16; Psalm 66:18) or what is good (cf. James 4:8; 1 Pet 1:22; 3:15; Prov 28:26; Col 3:15.) Regarding the soul's choice regarding affections, our Lord instructed,

Do not lay up for yourselves treasures on earth, where moth and rust destroy and where thieves break in and steal; but lay up for yourselves treasures in heaven, where neither moth nor rust destroys and where thieves do not break in and steal. For where your treasure is, there your heart will be also (Matt 6:19-21).

The apostle Paul admonishes,

If then you were raised with Christ, seek those things which are above, where Christ is, sitting at the right hand of God. Set your mind on things above, not on things on the earth (Col. 3:1,2).

The Spirit Chamber of the Heart

The "spirit chamber of the heart" has been made a new creation in Christ (2 Cor 5:17). This is the inner man that "delights in God's law" (Rom 7:22). The spirit/heart was cleansed by faith at salvation (Acts 15:9). This chamber is referred to in passages such Ezekiel's prophecy of regeneration:

Then I will sprinkle clean water on you, and you shall be clean; I will cleanse you from all your filthiness and from all your idols. *I will give you a new heart and put a new spirit within you*; I will take the heart of stone out of your flesh and give you a heart of flesh. I will put My Spirit within you and cause you to walk in My statutes, and you will keep My judgments and do them (Ezek 36:25-27).

Jeremiah also anticipated this heart change through the New Covenant:

But this is the covenant that I will make with the house of Israel after those days, says the LORD: *I will put My law in their minds, and write it on their hearts*; and I will be their God, and they shall be My people (Jer 31:33; cf. John 7:38; Matt. 12:35). [4]

As the believer knows and reckons true his identification with Christ, he appreciates his new heart, in which he has become a partaker of the divine nature (2 Pet 1:4).

This new heart calls us to love God supremely. The Song of Solomon portrays a poetic, Middle Eastern testimony of potential intimacy in godly married life. The bride declared,

Set me as a seal upon your *heart*, As a seal upon your arm; For love is as strong as death, Jealousy as cruel as the grave; Its flames are flames of fire, A most vehement flame. Many waters cannot quench love, Nor can the floods drown it. If a man would give for love All the wealth of his house, It would be utterly despised (Song 8:6,7).

As the Shulamite shared her heart with her groom, so the bride of Christ should reflect the Bridegroom's matchless love (2 Cor 11:2).

A United Heart

Our prayer should be for a united heart—one in which the "soul chamber" is in agreement with the "spirit chamber" in recognizing the worthiness of God. As the Psalmist prayed:

Teach me Your way, O LORD;
I will walk in Your truth;
Unite my heart to fear Your name."
(Psalm 86:11. cf. Eph 6:5; Col 3:22; Matt 22:37; Prov 3:5; Deut 11:13).

This model of understanding the heart has been helpful to students and counselees. I recall a testimony from a traineee in Brazil who publically testified of the new freedom she had been experiencing in light of these scriptural principles. This united heart will also promote peace and unity in Christian fellowship: "And let the peace of God rule in your hearts, to which also you were called in one body; and be thankful" (Col 3:15). Let us pray with David,

Let the words of my mouth
and the meditation of my heart
Be acceptable in Your sight,
O LORD, my strength and my Redeemer
(Psalm 19:14).

¹ Dr. M. R. De Haan, "Heart Trouble," *Our Daily Bread* (Grand Rapids: RBC Ministries, May 10, 1996).

² Ibid.

³ Jonathan Edwards, *Religious Affections*, part 1, chapter 2 (www. CCEL.org), [emphasis added].

⁴ Some have objected to this kind of personal emphasis on the New Covenant's promise of the believer's "new heart" (Ezek 36:26; Jer 31:31-34): "Ezekiel's promise of a new heart is part of a broader promise of Israel's restoration that includes other features not yet realized (Ezek. 36:22-36). The New Covenant promises begin to find their fulfillment in the New Testament, but none of these benefits are yet fully realized. From this perspective, Exchanged Life theology offers an overrealized eschatology"- Robert A. Pyne and Matthew L. Blackmon, "A Critique of the 'Exchanged Life.'" *Bibliotheca Sacra*, vol. 163, (April-June 2006), 151. However, one wonders why this covenant's final, comprehensive fulfillment in God's dealings with Israel negates the reality of the believer's new heart: "Therefore, if anyone is in Christ, he is a new creation; old things have passed away; behold, all things have become new" (2 Cor 5:17; cf. John 7:38). Just as the Abrahamic Covenant includes the blessings of the gospel to individual Gentiles (Gen 12:3; 15:6; Gal 3:5-14) even so the New Covenant includes the individual regeneration of believers in the covenant Christ ratified in His death and resurrection (Matt 26:28; 2 Cor 3:1-18). For further study on the qualities of this new heart, see Dwight Edwards, *Revolution Within: A Fresh Look at Supernatural Living* (Colorado Springs, CO: Waterbrook, 2001); Frank Allnutt, *The Christian's New Heart* (FrankAllnutt.com); Oswald Chambers, *Biblical Psychology* (Grand Rapids: Discovery House Publishers, 1995), 91-133.

SELECTED BIBLIOGRAPHY

SELECTED BIBLIOGRAPHY

Bauer, W., W. Arndt, and F. W. Gingrich. *Greek-English Lexicon of the New Testament.* University of Chicago Press, 1958.

Brown, Colin ed. *The New International Dictionary of New Testament Theology.* Exeter: Paternoster Press, 1975. S.v. "Soul," "Spirit."

Brown, F., S. R. Driver, and C. A. Briggs. *A Hebrew and English Lexicon to the Old Testament.* Oxford University Press, 1957.

Cremer, Herman. *Biblical-Theological Lexicon of the New Testament Greek.* trans. William Urwick, Edinburgh: T. & T. Clark, 1895.

Douglas, J.D. ed. *The New Bible Dictionary.* Wheaton: Tyndale House, 1962.

Hamel, Ken. *The Online Bible.* Online Bible Software, 2000.

Harris, R. Laird, Gleason L. Archer and Bruce K. Walke. *Theological Wordbook of the Old Testament.* Chicago: Moody Press, 1980.

Hewitt, Thomas. *The Epistle to the Hebrews.* Tyndale New Testament Commentaries. vol. 15, ed. R. V. G. Tasker, London: Intervarsity Press, 1974.

The Holy Bible. New King James Version.

Jackson, Samuel ed. *The New Schaff–Herzog Encyclopedia of Religious Knowledge.* NY: Funk and Wagnalls, 1911.

Jamieson, Robert, A. R. Fausset, and David Brown. *Commentary on the Whole Bible.* Revised ed., Grand Rapids: Zondervan, 1961.

Kittel, Gerhard and Gerhard Friedrich eds. *Theological Dictionary of the New Testament.* trans. Geoffrey Bromiley. Grand Rapids: Eerdmans, 1964.

Lenski, R. C. H. *The Interpretation of St. Paul's Epistles to the Thessalonians* Minneapolis, MN: Augsburg, 1964.

Loyd-Jones, D. Martin. Romans: *The New Man.* vol. 6, Grand Rapids: Zondervan, 1972.

Murray, John. *The Epistle to the Romans.* Grand Rapids: Eerdmans, 1968.

Orr, James ed. *The International Standard Bible Encyclopedia.* Grand Rapids: Eerdmans, 1939.

Scofield, C. I. ed. *The Scofield Reference Bible.* NY: Oxford University Press, 1909.

Tenney, Merrill C. ed., *The Zondervan Pictorial Encyclopedia of the Bible.* Grand Rapids; Zondervan, 1975.

Thayer, Joseph Henry. *Greek–English Lexicon of the New Testament.* Grand Rapids: Baker, 1977.

Trench, Richard C. *Synonyms of the New Testament.* Grand Rapids: Eerdmans, 1963.

Vine, W. E. *Expository Dictionary of New Testament Words.* Westood, NJ: Flemming H. Revell, 1940.

Wooton, R. W. F. "Spirit and Soul in the New Testament." *The Bible Translator* 26 (1975), 239-44.

Counseling

A Comprehensive Course in Effective Counseling. Oak Brook, IL: Institute in Basic Life Principles, n.d.

Adams, Jay E. *The Christian Counselor's Manual.* Grand Rapids: Baker Book House, 1973.

Burts, H. Greg. *Strategic Biblical Counseling.* Enumclaw, WA: Pleasant Word, 2004.

Corey, Gerald. *Theory and Practice of Counseling and Psychotherapy.* Monterey, CA: Brooks/Cole Publishing Co., 1977.

Crabb, Lawrence J. Jr. *Effective Biblical Counseling.* Grand Rapids: Zondervan Publishing House, 1977.

Hunter, Rodney J. ed. *Dictionary of Pastoral Care and Counseling.* Nashville: Abingdon Press, 1990.

Hyder, O. Quentin. *The Christian's Handbook of Psychiatry.* Old Tappan, NJ: Fleming H. Revell, 1971.

MacArthur, John Jr. *The Sufficiency of Christ.* Dallas: Word Publishing, 1991.

Minirth, Frank B. *Christian Psychiatry.* Old Tappan, NJ: Revell, 1977.

Sanctification

Anderson, Neil. *Victory Over the Darkness.* Ventura, CA: Regal Books, 1990.

Anderson, Neil, and Robert L. Saucy. *The Common Made Holy.* Eugene, OR: Harvest House Publishers, 1997.

Edman, V. Raymond. *They Found the Secret.* Grand Rapids: Zondervan Publishing House, 1960.

Fromke, DeVern. *Ultimate Intention.* Indianapolis, IN: Sure Foundation, 1963.

Gillham, Bill. *Lifetime Guarantee.* Eugene, OR: Harvest House, 1993.

Hall, Richard. *Foundations of Exchanged Life Counseling.* Aurora, CO: Cross-Life Publications, 1993.

Hopkins, Evan H. *The Law of Liberty in the Spiritual Life.* American ed. Fort Washington, PA: Christian Literature Crusade, 1991.

Huegel, F. J. *Bone of His Bone.* Grand Rapids: Zondervan Publishing House. 1972.

Nee, Watchman. *The Spiritual Man.* NY: Christian Fellowship Publishers, 1968.

Needham, David. *Alive for the First Time.* Sisters, OR: Questar Publishers, 1995.

_____. *Birthright.* Portland, OR: Multnomah Press, 1979.

Olford, Stephen F. *Not I, But Christ.* Wheaton, IL: Crossway Books, 1995.

Solomon, Charles. *Handbook to Happiness.* Wheaton, Il: Tyndale 1982.

_____. *Handbook for Christ-Centered Counseling* [previous edition: *Counseling with the Mind of Christ*]. Old Tappan, NJ: Revell, 1977.

Solomon, Charles, Stoney Shaw, and John Woodward, *The Solomon Institute in Spirituotherapy.* Sevierville, TN: Grace Fellowship, 2001.

Stanford, Miles. *The Complete Green Letters.* Grand Rapids: Zondervan, 1975.

Taylor, Howard and Geraldine. *Hudson Taylor's Spiritual Secret.* Chicago: Moody Press, 1932.

Thomas, W. Ian. *The Mystery of Godliness.* Grand Rapids: Zondervan, 1964.

Towns, Elmer L. *Understanding the Deeper Life.* Old Tappan, NJ: Revell, 1988.

Wells, Michael. *Sidetracked in the Wilderness.* Grand Rapids: Fleming H. Revell, 1991.

History

Douglas, J. D., ed. *The New International Dictionary of the Christian Church.* Revised ed. Grand Rapids: Zondervan, 1978.

Ferguson, Everett. *Encyclopedia of Early Christianity.* 2nd. ed. NY: Garland Publishers, 1997.

Guyon, Jeanne. *Experiencing the Depths of Jesus Christ.* ed. Gene Edwards. Goleta, CA: Christian Books, 1975.

Luther, Martin. *Luther's Works.* vol.21, ed., J. Pelikan. St. Louis: Concordia, 1956.

Walker, Williston. *A History of the Christian Church.* New York: Charles Scribner's Sons, 1970.

Theology

Austin-Sparks, T. *What is Man?* Cloverdale, IN: Ministry of Life, n. d.

Berkhof, L. *Systematic Theology.* Grand Rapids: Eerdmans, 1939.

Bernard, Thomas D. *The Progress of Doctrine in the New Testament.* Grand Rapids: Eerdmans, 1949.

Boyd, Jeffrey H. "One's Self Concept and Biblical Theology." *Journal of the Evangelical Theological Society* 40. (1997): 207-27.

Barackman, Floyd H. *Practical Christian Theology*. Old Tappan, NJ: Fleming H. Revell, 1981.

Buswell, James O. *A Systematic Theology of the Christian Religion*. Grand Rapids: Zondervan, 1962.

Cambron, Mark. *Bible Doctrine*. Grand Rapids: Zondervan, 1954.

Chafer, Lewis S. *Systematic Theology*. Dallas, TX: Dallas Seminary Press, 1947.

Chambers, Oswald. *Biblical Psychology*. 2d ed. Grand Rapids: Discovery House, 1995.

Clark, Gordon H. *The Biblical Doctrine of Man*. Jefferson, MD: The Trinity Foundation, 1984.

Delitzsch, Franz. *A System of Biblical Psychology*. Edinburgh: T. & T. Clark, 1867.

Elwell, Walter ed. *Evangelical Dictionary of Biblical Theology*. Grand Rapids: Baker Book House, 1996.

Enns, Paul. *The Moody Handbook of Theology*. Chicago: Moody, 1989.

Erickson, Millard J. *Christian Theology*. Grand Rapids: Baker, 1983.

Fitzwater, P. B. *Christian Theology*. Grand Rapids: Eerdmans, 1948.

Fowler, James. *Toward a Christian Understanding of Man*. www.ChristInYou.net, 2002.

Grudem, Wayne. *Systematic Theology*. Grand Rapids: Zondervan, 1994.

Harrison, Everett F. ed. *Baker's Dictionary of Theology*. Grand Rapids: Baker Book House, 1960.

Heard, J. B. *The Tripartite Nature of Man.* Edinburgh: T. & T. Clark, 1875.

Hodge, Charles. *Systematic Theology.* Grand Rapids: Eerdmans, 1979.

Hoekema, Anthony A. *Created in God's Image.* Grand Rapids: Eerdmans, 1986.

Holdcroft, L. Thomas. *Anthropology: A Biblical View.* Clayburn, BC: Cee Picc, 1990.

Jennings, George J. "Some Comments on the Soul." *Journal of the American Scientific Affiliation,* 19 (1967): 7-11.

Jones, Gordon Scott. *Fundamental Man: The Doctrine of Anthropology.* www.BibleRevival.com/ReadingRoom.htm

Lewis Gordon R. and Bruce A. Demarest. *Integrative Theology.* Grand Rapids: Zondervan, 1990.

Lockyer, Herbert. *All the Doctrines of the Bible.* Grand Rapids: Zondervan, 1964.

Milne, Bruce. *Know the Truth.* Downers Grove, IL: Inter Varsity Press, 1982.

Moody, Dale. *The Word of Truth.* Grand Rapids: Eerdmans, 1981.

Oehler, Gustav F. *Theology of the Old Testament.* trans. George E. Day. NY: Funk and Wagnalls, 1883.

Pember, G. H. *Earth's Earliest Ages.* Grand Rapids: Kregel Publications, 1942.

Penn-Lewis, Jessie. *Soul and Spirit: A Glimpse into Biblical Psychology.* Fort Washington, PA: Christian Literature Crusade, 1992.

Reinhold, Roy A., *The Nature of Man.* www.ad2004.com, 2005.

Richards, Lawrence O. and Gib Martin. *A Theology of Personal Ministry: Spiritual Giftedness in the Local Church.* Grand Rapids: Zondervan, 1981.

Spurrier, William A. *Guide to the Christian Faith.* New York: Charles Scribner's Sons, 1952.

Sheldon, Henry C. *A System of Christian Doctrine.* Boston: Carl H. Heintzemann, 1900.

Strong, Augustus H. *Systematic Theology.* Philadelphia: Fortess Press, 1907.

Terry, Milton S. *Biblical Dogmatics: An Exposition of the Principal Doctrines of the Holy Scriptures.* NY: Eaton and Mains, 1907.

Thiessen, Henry C. *Introductory Lectures in Systematic Theology.* Grand Rapids: Wm. B. Eerdmans, 1949.

MAN AS SPIRIT, SOUL AND BODY:

SCRIPTURE INDEX

A STUDY OF BIBLICAL PSYCHOLOGY

SCRIPTURE INDEX

REFERENCE	PAGE
GENESIS	
Gen 1:24	96
Gen 1:26	34
Gen 1:26,27	46, 85, 87
Gen 1:28	25
Gen 1:31	25
Gen 2:7	8, 9, 23, 34, 46, 47, 53, 67, 88
Gen 2:16,17	47, 48, 86, 99
Gen 2:19	34, 96
Gen 2:21	38
Gen 2:30	34
Gen 3:14-19	48
Gen 3:15,21	86
Gen 3:19	24
Gen 5:5	48
Gen 6:3	38
Gen 6:12	38
Gen 7:15	17
Gen 8:1	30
Gen 12:3	152
Gen 15:6	152
Gen 18:5	40
Gen 35:18	5, 8, 31, 34

REFERENCE	PAGE
Gen 37:27	38
Gen 41:8	8
EXODUS	
Ex 10:13	30
Ex 15:8	30
Ex 15:9	35
Ex 25-31	11
Ex 36:2	40
LEVITUCUS	
Lev 17:11	34
Lev 19:18	100
Lev 21:1-14	98
Lev 24:18	96
NUMBERS	
Num 5:2	35
Num 5:14	30
Num 6:6	35, 96
Num 8:7	38
Num 11:17	31
Num 11:25	31
Num 12:1	8

REFERENCE	PAGE	REFERENCE	PAGE
Ps 51:10	62	**ISAIAH**	
Ps 56:4	38	Isa 9:6	141
Ps 66:18	149	Isa 10:8	34
Ps 78:8	49	Isa 11:2	31
Ps 86:4	35	Isa 25:4	30
Ps 86:11	151	Isa 31:33	38
Ps 86:13	31	Isa 32:15	31
Ps 104:25,29	30	Isa 40:31	115
Ps 104:29	17	Isa 42:1	31
Ps 104:30	31	Isa 42:5	30
Ps 107:9	35	Isa 46:2	35
Ps 143:10	31	Isa 54:6	30
		Isa 57:15	30
PROVERBS		Isa 59:1	86
Prov 3:5	151	Isa 59:2	49, 86
Prov 4:23	10, 147	Isa 61:1	31
Prov 20:27	48, 92		
Prov 23:17	35	**JEREMIAH**	
Prov 25:23	30	Jer 2:24	35
Prov 28:26	149	Jer 5:9	35, 104
		Jer 6:8	104
ECCLESIASTES		Jer 17:9	49, 149
Eccl 3:21	6, 17	Jer 31:31-34	152
Eccl 7:8	30	Jer 31:33	150
Eccl 12:7	31	Jer 49:36	30
SONG OF SOLOMON		**EZEKIEL**	
Song 1:7	35	Ezek 11:19	31
Song 3:1-4	35	Ezek 36:22-36	152
Song 8:6,7	151	Ezek 36:25	150
		Ezek 36:26,27	31, 150, 152

REFERENCE	PAGE	REFERENCE	PAGE
Luke 10:22	41	ACTS	
Luke 10:27	100	Acts 2:17	40
Luke 11:34	92	Act 2:41	36
Luke 12:22	36	Acts 2:43	36
Luke 13:11	144	Acts 3:23	36
Luke 16:19-31	64	Acts 14:2	96
Luke 16:24	23	Acts 15:9	150
Luke 21:34	41	Acts 16:4	41
Luke 23:43	6	Acts 17:28	47
Luke 24:4	102	Acts 17:32	7
Luke 24:37,39	33	Acts 20:10	36
		Acts 23:1	41
JOHN		Acts 23:8,9	99
John 1:13	11, 50	Acts 28:22	41
John 3:3-8	50		
John 3:6	40	ROMANS	
John 3:8	32	Rom 1:4	32
John 4:23	52, 84, 139	Rom 1:18-20	85
John 4:24	47, 52, 104, 139	Rom 1:24	41
		Rom 2:14	86
John 5:28,29	65	Rom 2:15	10, 86
John 6:63	40	Rom 5:5	41
John 7:38	150, 152	Rom 5:10	116
John 10:11	36	Rom 5:12	49
John 12:25	37	Rom 6-8	60, 103
John 12:27	53, 96	Rom 6:3-7	60
John 13:21	96	Rom 6:6	58, 60, 63, 120
John 14:1	10		
John 14:26	33	Rom 6:11	60
John 15:1-8	116	Rom 6:12,13	25, 39
John 15:26	33	Rom 6:13	63
John 16:12-15	141	Rom 7:5	40
John 18:39	41	Rom 7:7-24	50

REFERENCE	PAGE	REFERENCE	PAGE
Rom 7:14	59	1 Cor 2:12	58, 86
Rom 7:14-24	61	1 Cor 2:13	59, 86
Rom 7:15-8:11	140	1 Cor 2:14	34, 49, 59, 66, 84, 86, 94, 101
Rom 7:24	52		
Rom 7:17-23	101	1 Cor 2:14,15	101
Rom 7:17	51, 81, 83	1 Cor 2:15-3:1	58
Rom 7:18	40, 51, 149	1 Cor 3:2,3	58
Rom 7:22	62, 98, 150	1 Cor 3:16	87, 96
Rom 7:24	49, 52	1 Cor 4:21	32
Rom 8:1	59	1 Cor 5:3	8
Rom 8:4,5	33	1 Cor 5:5	96, 97
Rom 8:9	33	1 Cor 6:13	39
Rom 8:11	96	1 Cor 6:17	52, 84, 97, 98, 104
Rom 8:15	32		
Rom 8:16	18, 52, 84, 97, 104, 139	1 Cor 6:19	39, 87
		1 Cor 7:3-5	25
Rom 8:23	97	1 Cor 7:14	39
Rom 8:30	65	1 Cor 7:37	11
Rom 9:3	40	1 Cor 9:27	25, 39, 63
Rom 11:8	32	1 Cor 14:2	84
Rom 12:2	10, 97, 99	1 Cor 14:14	84, 101
Rom 12:3	41	1 Cor 14:15,16	84
Rom 12:5	38	1 Cor 15:35-55	65
Rom 12:11	84, 148	1 Cor 15:37,40	38
Rom 14:20-24	86	1 Cor 15:39	40
		1 Cor 15:42-44	65
1 CORINTHIANS		1 Cor 15:44	16, 101
1 Cor 1:2	98	1 Cor 15:44,46	34
1 Cor 1:9	86	1 Cor 15:45	36, 47, 52
1 Cor 1:26	40	1 Cor 15:45-48	65
1 Cor 2:11	8, 17, 53, 58, 96	1 Cor 15:47	52
		1 Cor 15:51	53
1 Cor 2:11-14	89	1 Cor 16:18	98

Man As Spirit, Soul, and Body

REFERENCE	PAGE	REFERENCE	PAGE
2 CORINTHIANS		**EPHESIANS**	
2 Cor 3:1-18	152	Eph 1:13,19	51
2 Cor 4:6	41	Eph 2:1	49, 52, 86
2 Cor 4:13	32	Eph 2:1-8	97
2 Cor 5:1-4	24	Eph 2:5	49, 52
2 Cor 5:6	24	Eph 2:6	88
2 Cor 5:6-8	63	Eph 2:8-10	117
2 Cor 5:7	49	Eph 2:10	51
2 Cor 5:8	6, 24	Eph 2:13	88
2 Cor 5:12	41	Eph 3:1-10	53
2 Cor 5:17	51, 120, 150, 152	Eph 4:17,18	49
		Eph 4:19	49
2 Cor 7:1	33, 98	Eph 5:28	39
2 Cor 9:7	41	Eph 6:5	40, 151
2 Cor 10:5	94	Eph 6:6	36
2 Cor 11:2	151	Eph 6:10	99
2 Cor 12:2,3	39	Eph 6:10-18	143, 145
2 Cor 12:9	140	Eph 6:22	41
2 Cor 12:18	32		
2 Cor 13:14	87	**PHILIPPIANS**	
		Phil 1:21,22	63
GALATIANS		Phil 1:23,24	6
Gal 2:20	40, 115, 116, 118, 140	Phil 1:23	24, 37, 63
		Phil 1:27	32
Gal 3:5-14	152	Phil 2:13	51
Gal 5:16	50, 58	Phil 3:3	52
Gal 5:17	58	Phil 3:20,21	65, 97
Gal 5:19-21	58	Phil 4:4	97
Gal 5:22	62		
Gal 6:15	51	**COLOSSIANS**	
		Col 1:27	87
		Col 2:23	39

Man As Spirit, Soul, and Body